SPECTACULAR CANADIANS

Weird, Wild and Wonderful

A.H. Jackson

BLUE
BIKE
BOOKS

The Publisher: Blue Bike Books
Website: www.bluebikebooks.com

Library and Archives Canada Cataloguing in Publication

Jackson, A.H., 1944–
    Spectacular Canadians: weird, wild and wonderful / A.H. Jackson.

ISBN 978-1-926700-34-2

    1. Canada—Biography. 2. Canada—Miscellanea. I. Title.

FC25.J33 2011   920.071   C2011-903225-2

Project Director: Nicholle Carrière
Project Editor: Nicholle Carrière
Cover Images: Roger Garcia, Patrick Hénaff, Roly Wood, Photos.com
Illustrations: Roger Garcia, Patrick Hénaff, Peter Tyler, Djordje Todorovic, Roly Wood
Photo Credits: Every effort has been made to accurately credit the sources of photographs. Any errors or omissions should be reported directly to the publisher for correction in future editions. Photographs courtesy of Glenbow Museum (p. 25, NA-1506-1; p. 28, NA-1258-123; p. 117, NA-2539-19; p. 173, NA-239-25; p. 179, NA-165-4; p. 183, NA-2745-1; p. 191, NA-3082-4; p. 200, NA-5600-8302b); International Communications Systems (pp. 87, 91); Library of Congress (pp. 37, 40, 77, 79, 125); National Archives of Canada (p. 14, C-44702); Vancouver Public Library, Special Collections (p. 111, VPL 22860); WikiCommons (p. 188).

Produced with the assistance of the Government of Alberta, Alberta Multimedia Development Fund

Government of Alberta ■

We acknowledge the financial support of the Government of Canada through the Canada Book Fund (CBF) for our publishing activities.

■✦■ Canadian Heritage   Patrimoine canadien

PC: 5

CONTENTS

DEDICATION

This book is for William "Billy" Jamieson, who is off exploring
on a higher plane

INTRODUCTION

The *Oxford Dictionary* defines *weird* as "pertaining to the bizarre or the supernatural" and offers as an example of modern-day usage the phrase "all those weird and wonderful characters." This example almost begs inclusion of the word *Canadian* because, of all the nations on this planet, no other has owed so much to so many weird and wonderful characters as Canada. That most of these individuals hailed from other places is of no consequence because once they arrived here, those weird and wonderful people turned to nation building, and while many had come to take, most stayed to give back, an ongoing process that makes for interesting history that is unlike that taught to school children.

Around 12,000 years ago, Canada and the whole of North America was a clean slate, completely empty of people, but it had something that attracted a few weird, wild and wonderful Eurasians—a very large food supply in the now-extinct woolly mammoth. The Eurasians came, ate big until big was no more and stayed to become the indigenous tribes of North America. This was fortuitous for modern-day Canadians because those early nation builders hybridized the corn that enabled Europeans to push west, for without that staple crop, there would have been no fur trade and probably no Canada. The adventurers that arrived to construct those famous fur-trading posts in Canada's wilderness subsisted on a diet of game, fish and corn, which had its hard outer shell removed by boiling the kernels in a lye solution. Freed from their outer husk, the corn kernels were then rinsed numerous times, dried in the sun and ground into hominy, commonly called "Indian meal." Trappers, traders, settlers and anyone going west from Montréal or Québec City stocked up on as many barrels of Indian meal as they could stuff into their wagons. First Nations tribes, specifically the Iroquois of the Mohawk Nation, supplied the corn, but also provided an element of danger. Fur trading was a lucrative enough enterprise to attract a plethora of weird, wild and wonderful characters. Initially, they were French businessmen (whom historians like to call explorers) calling themselves the Canada and Acadia Company, but the reality is much different, as the only thing those men were exploring was a way to get cheap beaver pelts to replace those from Russia, which had become rare and expensive. Felt hats were becoming the rage in Europe, and the demand for more beaver pelts for felting had become huge.

Beginning in 1600, the Canada and Acadia Company made feeler voyages to Canada, and each voyage returned with enough pelts to spur on the next year's trip. The company's 1604 venture, led for the second time by Samuel de Champlain, caused the company to forget about cheap pelts and recognize the danger that was the Iroquois. While attempting to trade with a hunting party of Iroquois at the Bay of Fundy, de Champlain's group came under attack and several men were killed. After burying their dead, de Champlain and his men were rowing back to their ship when the Iroquois emerged from the forest, dug up the buried corpses and, after roasting them on open fires, ate them in full view of de Champlain and his crew. After all, the Iroquois were part of the Mohawk Nation, and, in their language, the word *mohawk* means "eaters of flesh." From that point on, the fur trade with Canada's indigenous peoples was conducted from secure forts with guns at the ready, a slow and rather expensive undertaking. However, with European hat makers willing to pay a king's ransom for every beaver pelt, dealing with cannibal tribes was just another problem to overcome. French nobles and businessmen quickly formed a new and larger concern, the Company of One Hundred Associates, to establish a fortified town at the place where the St. Lawrence River narrows, which they called Tadoussac.

It was a good plan, except for three things, or rather three individuals—the Kirke brothers. England and France were at war, and British business interests, not wanting the French to have free reign in Canada, formed the Knights Baronet of Nova Scotia, outfitted three warships, and in 1628, put them under the command of David, Louis and Thomas Kirke, three seafaring brothers with an English father and French mother. As luck would have it, the brothers' well-armed ships sought shelter from a storm at the Gaspé, where they discovered 24 mostly unarmed French ships ferrying men and supplies to de Champlain's fort at Tadoussac. The French captains surrendered, and the Kirkes sent them to England along with their ships, which they claimed as spoils of war. Although the Kirkes were unable to dislodge de Champlain from Tadoussac, they did capture a second French supply convoy. This put Québec at the brothers' mercy when they returned from England in the summer of 1629 (see the Our Kings of Canada section).

Present-day Canada is huge, but in the 17th century, our nation consisted of only a few beaches in Newfoundland, Nova Scotia and New Brunswick, along with a big river that had no name except that of a bay named by Jacques Cartier on Saint Lawrence's Day in 1535. Nobody much cared about the river until European hatters forced its exploration at the start of the next century. The commodity that people fought over at the time, and for centuries afterward, swam in the coastal waters of Newfoundland—the stockfish. European cities depended on cod, haddock and mackerel, and they fought many wars for the right to fish in North Atlantic waters, confrontations that caused fishing fleets to brave dangerous seas and move operations to Newfoundland. For a time, Basque,

English, French, Spanish and Dutch fishermen all had a little piece of the big island, a land governed by "fishing admirals." The master of the first ship into harbour became the port admiral and dispensed rough justice until the next season. This weird legal system favoured fishermen over settlers and maintained the island as the private preserve of merchants and fishermen. It eventually degenerated into a haven for pirates, with one of the greatest being the legendary Captain Peter Easton. Easton, a virtual nobody to historians, is one of the most successful bad guys in the annals of Maritime plundering, and for many years, he was the outright ruler of Canada (you can read more about him in the Our Kings of Canada section).

Salt fish was the great enabler that allowed Europeans a toe-hold in Canada, and with more than enough fish for all, the various nationalities got along famously. Basque fishermen salted their catch onboard and returned home to dry it, and while the French and English both salted and dried fish on New World beaches, they did so far enough away from each other to avoid contact. They worked for businessmen, and following the motto "Live and let live" was good for profit. It was a system that worked well until the mid-18th century, when French and English trading began to conflict, resulting in several small military engagements. The most notable of these was General George Washington's 1754 attack on a small troop of Canadians and the suspected assassination of their leader, Joseph Coulon de Villiers de Jumonville.

Sanctioned by Virginia Royal Governor John Dinwiddie without assent from Britain, this incident helped ignite the infamous Seven Year War between France and England, often referred to as the French and Indian War. This conflict would end France's New World colonial aspirations and signal the beginning of the great British business venture called Canada.

From 1760 until well into the 20th century, British business interests governed every aspect of life in Canada—trees were cut to build British ships and homes, fish were caught to supply the home country and its traders, and animals, especially beavers, were trapped for their pelts, which were used to make hats and coats for British gents and ladies. Almost all new businesses and westward expansion depended on British investment, and Canada became a destination for the younger sons of those wealthy British investors. Historians call them "remittance men" because they depended on a family allowance for survival and were freed from the necessity of working for their daily bread. From these thousands of remittance men, Canada would reap a harvest of weird and wonderful adventurers, young guys with time on their hands to explore, to chart unknown territories and to become politicians, entrepreneurs, pirates and even would-be kings.

During most of the 20th century, almost the entire mineral, agricultural and industrial output of Canada was devoted to supplying Britain in its war efforts and post-war economic recoveries. If Canada did not make, grow or mine what Britain needed, Britain sent the wherewithal and expertise to get it and re-created Canada as the world's biggest business, setting the stage for our weird and wild entrepreneurs to departmentalize and own that business. Today, as it was in times past, Canada's vast mineral, forest, agricultural and industrial output is mostly owned by conglomerates run by a few weird and wonderful characters aspiring to be kings, and good or bad, it is an age-old system familiar to all Canadians.

Our Kings of Canada

In 1534, Jacques Cartier claimed Canada for the
King of France, but this action was incidental to his
raison d'être—to find a passage to the Orient. Cartier
returned to France that same year believing he had
reached a forgotten edge of the East, only to change
his mind during his voyages of 1535 and 1541. He
had indeed found a new land, and though Cartier
claimed it for France, he found its inhabitants less than
amenable to subjugation and good at shooting arrows.
He ultimately decided that it should be politicized
before colonization.

Subsequent agents of the French king did not share
Cartier's views and arrived full of bravado, bristling
with guns and ready to subdue all the indigenous
peoples through military force and religious undertakings. Samuel de Champlain had a go as well, but only
succeeded in making enemies and was eventually run off

in 1628 by the Kirke brothers, three French Huguenot privateers who held a different outlook regarding the new land.

Led by the eldest brother, David, the Kirkes had little interest in colonization; they worked for English businessmen and were after profit from fish, furs and whatever else they could find, an attitude adopted by those who came after and misinterpreted by historians to mean exploration for the sake of knowledge. To the indigenous peoples of Canada and the businessmen in Europe, explorers were simply scouts for the armies that followed; they mapped, noted opportunities and established parameters for future profit.

SIR DAVID KIRKE
1597–1654
The Great Pirate Admiral

The eldest of three Huguenot brothers, David Kirke was
a French Protestant with an urge to damage the French
Catholic regime of Cardinal Richelieu. He was also of a mind
to put a dent in the profits of the Company of the Hundred
Associates, the French trading company financing Samuel
Champlain's trading settlement at Tadoussac on the
St. Lawrence, where it meets the Saguenay River.

History will mark David Kirke as being audacious, lucky and
the pirate who became the absolute ruler of Canada for many
years. David's father, a well-to-do London merchant, had the
money and connections necessary to supply his sons with
three well-armed ships to blockade the St. Lawrence River
and force the French from Canada. Just a pipe dream, because
de Champlain had fortified Tadoussac and could endure an
attack from twice that many vessels. However, Lady Luck took
a hand when the Kirke ships, on their way up the river to
Tadoussac, sought refuge from a storm in the same bay as
a mostly unarmed French supply fleet. The French fleet surrendered and was sent to England as war booty. This was all
fortuitous for Kirke, but it still left him unable to dislodge
de Champlain from Tadoussac—the settlement was simply too
well fortified. Sailing back down the St. Lawrence on his
return voyage to England, Kirke once again felt the hand of
Lady Luck when he encountered another lightly armed French
supply fleet and captured it. David Kirke now possessed the
key to unlock Tadoussac, and the next year, 1628, he sailed
into Tadoussac knowing that his demands for de Champlain's
surrender would not be ignored because the inhabitants
were starving.

David Kirke returned home in 1629, but he left Québec under the control of his brother, who sent huge shipments of furs and dried fish home to be split between his father's company and King Charles I. In 1632, King Charles returned Québec to the French, and as compensation, David Kirke was knighted, received a coat of arms (now the coat of arms of Newfoundland and Labrador) and his father's company was given a Royal Charter that granted them possession of the island of Newfoundland with David Kirke as proprietary governor, a job for which he was eminently suited.

Kirke fortified the main settlement of Ferryland at the head of the Avalon Peninsula, renamed the island Pool Plantation, instituted a court of law, brought in colonists, taxed fishermen and supply boats, and behaved pretty much like he was the "King of Canada" until his luck ran out in 1651. Recalled to England on trumped-up charges laid by fish merchants intent on blocking his colonization projects, Kirke was tossed into prison and is thought to have died there in 1654. However, his wife, Lady Sarah Kirke, and their three sons carried on running Pool Plantation and became the new "rulers" of Canada until, in 1665 and 1672, Dutch raiders from New Amsterdam (present-day New York City) reduced the family's property holdings to the area around their fortified town of Ferryland on the Avalon Peninsula.

The Kirke family dominated the salt fish business in Newfoundland until 1696, when a final French raid all but wiped out the English fishing industry on the island.

SIR GEORGE SIMPSON
1797–1860
Canada's Little Emperor

Sir George Simpson, while still in his thirties, rose through the ranks of the Hudson's Bay Company (HBC) to become governor-in-chief of Rupert's Land in 1820, and never was there a man more properly placed. Simpson took what had, over the years, become a less-than-profitable venture and put it back on the money road. Under his steadying hand, Rupert's Land grew to include the entire northwest of Canada, the Alaska Panhandle and the Oregon Country down to the 45th parallel. Simpson ruled Rupert's Land with all the power of an Old World monarch; he made laws, enforced them and brooked no interference from anyone. As one Hudson's Bay factor wrote of Sir George:

In no colony subject to the British Crown is there to be found an authority so despotic as is at this day exercised in the mercantile Colony of Rupert's Land; and authority combining the despotism of military rule with the strict surveillance and mean parsimony of the avaricious trade. From Labrador to Nootka Sound the unchecked, uncontrolled will of a single individual gives law to the land…Clothed with a power so unlimited, it is not to be wondered at that a man who rose from a humble situation should in the end forget what he was and play the tyrant.

As virtual ruler of Canada, Simpson was above the law, especially when it came to marriage, and in 1890, he abandoned his wife and two children to marry his cousin without first getting divorced. This second liaison produced five children, and in later years, Simpson would father five more with several other wives of convenience.

In 1841, after receiving a knighthood from Queen Victoria, Sir George set off on an around-the-world tour. Travelling by horseback and canoe, he visited every HBC trading post in Canada, then took an HBC ship to Hawaii, where Simpson so impressed King Kamehameha III that he was appointed a king's envoy to Europe to secure international recognition for the Hawaiian kingdom.

Sir George "ruled" most of Canada and all of northern Ontario for over 40 years and was instrumental in the exploration and charting of a great deal of his domain. In 1857, a select committee of the British House of Commons investigating all facets of the HBC's activities in Canada called Sir George as a witness. He testified that Rupert's Land was unsatisfactory for settlement, but in the end, the committee recommended the annexation of the Red River Country and Saskatchewan into Canada.

KENNETH COLIN "KC" IRVING
1899–1992
The King of New Brunswick

KC Irving started out in 1923 selling cars in his hometown of Bouctouche, New Brunswick, and a year later, he owned his own dealership. Vehicles needed gas, so he opened service stations for Imperial Oil but was dealt a low blow when they decided to give his stations to someone else. No problem—he had good credit with his wealthy father, so he borrowed money and began building his own gas stations. He started his own construction company to build them, and when he was not building gas stations, he was constructing new homes. When Imperial Oil convinced the Canadian National Railway (CNR) to raise its tariff for shipping Irving's gasoline, he told them to get lost and bought ferries to transport his gas via the St. John River. More ferries needed to be built, so he bought a shipyard, and then a truck plant to transport his gas, and since both endeavours needed steel, he got into that business

as well. To remain independent of gasoline refiners, he collaborated with Chevron Oil, a U.S. company, to build a refinery in Saint John. Everything that KC Irving touched turned to gold, and it wasn't long before he discovered that he could turn politicians into gold simply by "touching" them with newsprint, and he soon owned every newspaper in New Brunswick.

KC Irving did not drink, smoke, swear or fool around on his wife—not much fun, but his self-discipline helped him create an empire of over 400 companies and made him the richest Canadian ever. Thoughts of Irving expanding beyond New Brunswick into the rest of Canada gnawed at the minds of Ottawa pundits like a beaver, but the pundits' concern was groundless as Irving was old school and thought New Brunswick was all the Canada he needed. Pity that, because of all the would-be kings of Canada, our weird, wild and wonderful KC Irving was one of the best.

PHILLIP ANDREW "RALPH" KLEIN
1917–
A Bridge Too Far

They called him "King Ralph" and his reign as premier of Alberta lasted from 1992 to 2006. Many Albertans loved him, but in Ottawa, the pundits were scared to death that his insistence on a balanced budget and health care would spread and make him King Ralph of Canada.

Born and educated in Calgary, Klein's first foray into the public eye was as the senior civic affairs reporter for CFCN-TV and CFCN Radio, a platform he used in 1980 to become mayor of Calgary. While mayor, he alienated a good portion of the country by promising to protect Calgary from the "bums and creeps" invading the city from central Canada, but in 1988, Calgary hosted the Winter Olympics and Klein's

KLEINOSAURUS

smiling face was everywhere, And, yes, he did support Brian Mulroney's conservatives, so the nation thought well of Ralph Klein.

Looking for bigger fish to fry, Klein jumped from civic to provincial politics. He won a seat in the Alberta Legislature, becoming the Honourable Ralph Klein, Minister of the Environment, where he soon garnered national attention by "flipping the bird" to an environmental activist. That reminded Albertans of Pierre Trudeau and his "fuddle duddle" remark, and they liked him for that. To protect Klein's image, his supporters even purchased the only existing photograph of him doing "the bird."

Image would become a problem for Ralph because he was a whisky-drinking man prone to overindulgence, especially after he became premier of Alberta on December 14, 1992. Alberta prospered like no other province, but Klein's proclivity for strong drink resulted in so many politically embarrassing situations that his public support began to dwindle, especially after 1993, when to balance the provincial books, he sold off the Alberta Energy Company without conducting a proper evaluation. In one instance, he was caught by the media lambasting a group of homeless people and tossing pocket change at them, and in 2003, when the first case of mad cow disease was discovered in Alberta, he blurted out that the rancher who owned the diseased cow should have buried the animal and kept his mouth shut. But Klein's most famous alcohol-induced faux pas occurred at a charity roast in 2009, when he pointed out guest MP Belinda Stronach, who had just deserted the Conservatives for the Liberal Party, and said, "Belinda roasted me as a Conservative, but, of course, now she's a Liberal. And I wasn't surprised she crossed over; I don't think she ever did have a Conservative bone in her body...well, except for one." He was, of course, referring to Stronach's former boyfriend, Conservative MP Peter MacKay.

Ralph Klein, who had a good shot at being King of Canada until torpedoed by his whisky mouth, saw his power erode until he just faded away in 2007. Today, Klein is a shadow of his former self—he was diagnosed with COPD, a lung disease, in December 2010, and a form of progressive dementia in April 2011.

DID YOU 🚪 KNOW?

Wrestling is popular in Mexico, especially when the match contestants, called *luchadores*, don colourful masks, with good guys fighting bad guys for supposed moral supremacy. A national phenomenon in Mexico, the masked *luchador* is a sports persona that wrestler Phil Klein, the father of former Alberta premier Ralph Klein, borrowed in the early 1950s when he donned a mask and fought all comers on the Stampede Wrestling circuit as "The Phantom."

Our
Soldiers

*After Confederation in 1867, Canada was a political
puppy of the British Parliament, which called the shots
on international affairs and defended the nation from
U.S. invasion. The fact is that Canadian Confederation
was a means by which the British could counter the
threat of attack by the Americans, with Britain supplying the military muscle to maintain the integrity of
Canada's borders.*

*In 1871, Britain withdrew its forces from Canada,
leaving the country's defence to local militia units, with
most being old boys' drinking clubs in which the wealthiest got to design the uniforms and yell out the orders.
Not a satisfactory situation for a nation still threatened
by the U.S., especially in the politically volatile West,
because the Americans had a large military presence
on the Prairies and planned to construct a railway
into Canada. That railway might have been the end of*

Canada's westward expansion were it not for an arrogant cavalryman named George Armstrong Custer and a cunning Sioux war chief named Sitting Bull. With the U.S. focusing its attention on avenging the Little Bighorn massacre, Canadian politicians hurriedly began the construction of a unifying railway through lands rife with American buffalo hunters, whisky traders, escaping Sioux, unruly First Nations tribes and the Métis. The Métis, who had a notion to form their own country, were the biggest threat to Canadian expansion, and to deal with them, Ottawa called out its boys' club militias.

The railway was already built, so transporting the militiamen was relatively easy, but fighting the Métis was not. However, even after the militias were dealt a few bloody noses, the railway kept bringing in such an overwhelming supply of men and guns that the Métis and their leader Louis Riel were overcome through attrition.

The Northwest Campaign was a major fiasco that left Ottawa politicians thinking that a regular army was needed. An opportunity to do that presented itself in 1880 when British Imperialists in South Africa went to war with the Boers. Canada sent a small volunteer army, the first real Canadian army, but the officers were still boys' club members. The war was another fiasco that would be repeated on a grander scale in 1899 with

the Second Boer War. Canada could not shake itself free of boys' club officers—after all, the British did it, and what was good for Britain was good for Canada. In 1914, the really big war in Europe cost our country almost 61,000 brave citizens, with most of them dying because of inept leadership from officers, a lesson learned and thankfully corrected by 1938, when officers were chosen for World War II and attained rank through military skills, training and battlefield merit, and not according to their social positions.

SIR ARTHUR WILLIAM CURRIE
1875–1933
The Butcher of Passchendaele

In 1914, the war department placed the grossly inexperienced Arthur Currie in command of a battalion and packed him off to battle the Germans, a job he embraced with all the aplomb of a Victoria, British Columbia, business executive. Currie was a politician's soldier, and by spending lives for results, he eventually rose to command all of Canada's forces in Europe. Historians write about the horrors of Passchendaele and expound on the glory of Vimy Ridge, but rarely do they dwell on the cost in human lives or on the man who hung back, spending those lives.

Canadian MP Sir Sam Hughes considered Currie a thoughtless butcher, and for his honesty in Parliament, Hughes became embroiled in a libel suit with Currie that caused financial problems for both. Needing money to stave off bankruptcy, Currie borrowed from regimental accounts, only to be rescued from an embezzlement charge by wealthy friends and from a court martial by the politicians he served so well. Currie would finish his days as president and vice-chancellor of McGill University, a post for which, like his military commands, he possessed absolutely no qualifications.

SAMUEL BENFIELD "SAM" STEELE
1849–1919
The Perfect Mountie

Anyone named Sam Steele has to be a fighter, and Steele was that in spades. Born in Purbrook, near Orillia, Ontario, he formed a militia unit to fight the Fenians when he was only 13 years old. Six years later, Steele joined the North-West

Mounted Police (NWMP) at its inception as recruit number three with the rank of sergeant major. In 1874, the government sent the Mounties west to control the U.S. whisky traders, a journey that turned into an unmitigated disaster, with deaths, desertions and starvation. The troop's leader, Commissioner George French, later heaped praise on Steele for his steadfast adherence to the job at hand.

In 1877, Steele, now a major, palavered with Chief Sitting Bull and tried unsuccessfully to convince him to return to the U.S., something Sitting Bull would do a few years later. In 1885, Steele was sent with two detachments of NWMP to help a group of cowboys and settlers defeat Chief Big Bear at the battle of Frenchman's Butte, at which they received a thrashing, and two years later, he was sent with a small detachment to Golden, British Columbia, to mediate problems between the indigenous peoples and the white settlers, a job he performed with tact, garnering kudos from both parties involved.

In 1892, Steele was promoted to commissioner and sent to the White and Chilicoot Passes to establish custom posts. After gold was discovered in the Klondike River in 1896, it was Steele who made the rule requiring prospectors to have a tonne of supplies before being allowed to cross. By 1898, Steele was in command of the NWMP in the Yukon and moved to clean up the lawless goldfield town of Dawson City, a big job made more difficult by the prevalence of guns, whisky and 14,000 newly rich, sometimes broke and always drunk residents. Steele took away their guns, but since he liked to gamble and drink whisky in the saloons, he left those establishments alone and just made sure the gamblers were honest.

Sam Steele was a regular guy and so highly regarded in Dawson that upon his recall, the entire town came to the docks to bid him adieu. Passed over for promotion, Steele quit the Mounties, and in 1900, he accepted command of CPR tycoon Lord Strathcona's Horse Regiment, a private "boys' club" light cavalry unit on its way to fight the Boers in South Africa and one that Sam quickly turned into a formidable fighting force.

At the conclusion of that war, Sam stayed in South Africa to command the "B" Division of the South African Constabulary, an army unit modelled after the NWMP. When World War I broke out in 1914, he volunteered, and though he was initially refused because of his age, he was later sent to England as an administrative commander. Canadian defence minister Samuel Hughes promoted Steele to brigadier general in command of all the Canadian forces in Europe in 1915, but the problem was that there was already a brigadier in charge of the troops, a conundrum that was not resolved until 1916, when the new defence minister relieved Steele after he refused to return home to become a recruiter. Steele hung onto his British command until he retired as a major general in 1918, receiving a knighthood and countless awards from Commonwealth and European countries.

Sam Steele, hard drinking, tough as nails, handy with a gun—a Mountie, soldier, peacekeeper and a weird and wonderful character who lived up to his name—was immortalized by his son, Harwood, in the bestselling novel, *Spirit of Iron*.

WILLIAM MAXWELL "MAX" AITKEN, LORD BEAVERBROOK
1879–1964
The Fixer

In 1940, the future of the free world was in the hands of Canadian-born industrialist Max Aitken, also known as Lord Beaverbrook, when Winston Churchill appointed him Minister for Aircraft Production. Britain had few fighter planes to oppose the onslaught of the Nazi Luftwaffe, and fighters would become Aitken's main concern. To acquire the parts necessary to build new planes and repair the old, he formed and sent out armed scavenger squads with orders to seize every aircraft part they could find and brook no interference from anyone. If a bomber sustained damage during a raid, its crew had to stand by helpless while Aitken's bandits quickly turned their aircraft into a truckload of spare parts.

Aitken dispersed fighter aircraft factories around England and ran them 24/7. In four months, he increased the monthly production of fighters from 183 to 471, and was repairing almost as many with scavenged parts.

This millionaire industrialist from Canada was a man with merit and true grit, who, along with his unsung scavenger squads, kept Commonwealth fighter pilots in the air long enough to win the Battle of Britain.

WILLIAM AVERY "BILLY" BISHOP
1894–1956
Canada's World War I Ace of Aces

Born in Owen Sound, Ontario, Billy Bishop followed his brother into Royal Military College and did rather poorly, having to repeat his first year. He was caught cheating during his third year and would have been tossed out but for the war. When World War I broke out in 1914, Billy joined the Mississauga Horse but was laid low by pneumonia and missed the boat to Europe. Transferred to the 7th Canadian Rifles, an infantry division from London, Ontario, Billy arrived in Europe the next year aboard a smelly cattle boat.

Billy did not take well to the life of an infantry officer, and to get free of the trenches, he transferred to the Royal Flying Corps, first as an observer and then as a flying officer. He busted up his knee on a training flight and missed the Battle of the Somme—a probable lifesaver. In March 1917, posted to No. 60 Squadron, Billy began downing enemy aircraft at an

exceptional rate, a fact he attributed to his skill at duck hunting, though some of his fellow pilots claimed that he simply
lied about his proficiency.

Billy was no stranger to lying and was caught in a few doozies,
most notably his fabricated account of having duelled with the
Red Baron and his claim of having shot down 25 enemy
planes in 23 days during his second tour at the front. As
a commanding officer during his second tour, Billy was per-
mitted to verify his own kills, a convenience that helped raise
his bag total to 67 enemy aircraft before he received the order
to stand down from fighting because politicians back in
Ottawa had begun to fear adverse public reaction should the
people's hero be shot down. Thinking it was all a load of
hooey, Billy disregarded the order and set off on one last mission in which he downed five more unconfirmed enemy
planes, bringing his total kills to 72, the most of any allied air-
man, though many military historians doubt the numbers.

Whatever the truth, Billy did shoot down plenty of enemy
planes, for which a grateful Canada and several European
countries awarded him a chest full of decorations, and from
Britain, he received the highest honour of all, the Victoria
Cross. During World War II, our "ace of aces," Billy Bishop,
was made Honorary Air Marshall of the RCAF in charge of
recruitment and air training.

Long gone, but still controversial, Billy once again made headlines in 2010, when Toronto "stole" his name from the Owen
Sound airport for their own downtown Island Airport. For
such an act of blatant thievery, many people half expected the
ghost of Billy Bishop to dive from the clouds in his little
fighter and strafe those pointy-headed Toronto politicos at the
renaming ceremony.

GEORGE FREDERICK "BUZZ" BEURLING
1921–48
Our Master of Malta

Intellectually, Buzz Beurling was never the sharpest knife in the drawer, but in an aircraft, he was master of the skies. During World War II, he became Canada's ace of aces, shooting down 31 enemy aircraft.

Born in Verdun, Québec, Buzz left school at an early age and took to the air flying freight out of Gravenhurst, Ontario. In 1937, he crossed into the U.S. as a visitor, and while he was attempting to volunteer for the Flying Tiger Corps to fight in China, he was declared an illegal alien and tossed into jail for several months. Deported back to Canada, he tried to join the Finnish Air Force to fight the Russians, but his application was rejected because his parents would not sign a permission slip.

When World War II broke out in 1939, Buzz offered his services to the RCAF, only to get a thumbs-down for his lack of education. Down but not out, he hopped a ship to England and volunteered for the RAF, only to be rejected yet again for not being able to supply a birth certificate. For that, he was forced to undertake a round trip to Montréal through submarine-infested waters, and upon returning in 1940 with the document, he was accepted into the RAF as a pilot sergeant. Posted to gunnery school, he spent long hours practising deflection and bullet drop techniques, and in the middle of December 1941, Buzz was posted to No. 403 Squadron to learn the intricacies of the Supermarine Spitfire and flew his first patrol on Christmas Day. In the spring, he joined the all-Canadian RCAF, and on May 1, 1942, he shot down his first enemy aircraft. He got another one two days later but broke formation to get it, for which he received a reprimand and the animosity of his mates. To make amends, he volunteered to fly in Malta, an island in the Mediterranean under intense attack by the German Air Force.

In Malta, Buzz was in his element, and by July 10, 1942, he had shot down five enemy aircraft to become an ace and a pilot officer with a Distinguished Flying Cross. By September, his kill tally had risen to 17, and he was shot down but not injured, something that would happen three more times in Malta. In October, with 27 kills to his credit, he was transferred back to England, but the transport plane crashed into the sea off Gibraltar, and Buzz incurred a serious leg injury.

Back in England, he was assigned to teach at gunnery school, but disciplinary problems such as fighting and being AWOL got him transferred around like a ping-pong ball, and he eventually ended up in the 412 Squadron, where he upped his kill tally to 31 and ran into more of the same disciplinary problems as before.

He was finally sent home, having achieved the rank of squadron leader, and the military had the idea to use him to sell war bonds. That plan ended with Buzz receiving an honourable discharge after a reporter asked him what he liked best about war, and Buzz replied, "Killing people."

After the war, Buzz did odd flying jobs, and in 1948, the new government of Israel put him under contract to deliver a P-51 Mustang and fly it for them. On the way, as Buzz was landing the plane in Italy, it inexplicably blew up, killing him. Sabotage was suspected. Buzz Beurling, Canada's World War II ace of aces who only lived for war, had finally used up his luck, and today, he rests in a military cemetery in Israel, a 100-percent Canadian hero who gave his life for Israel while looking for more people to kill.

DID YOU KNOW?

"Sentencing circles," a form of community justice employed by Canadian First Nations tribes, has become an accepted method of dispensing justice within the Canadian judicial system. First Nations people charged and found guilty of a crime may petition a provincial magistrate or judge for leave to be sentenced by a council comprised of community elders, the victim and the victim's family, the accused and the accused's family, along with a judge and defence counsel.

Tinkers, Tailors
and Candlestick Makers

*They were not itinerant fur traders; they were men
with families who came to Canada for the duration of
their lives. While most slipped into obscurity, a few of
these families endured, passing on financial and political legacies to form Canadian dynasties, of which there
are about 32, controlling almost half the gross national
product of the country. Exceptions to the dynasties are
the few recent immigrants who arrived with nothing but
made fortunes and the many immigrants who arrived
with fortunes, such as the Ghermezian family, who
came to Alberta from the U.S. via Iran. They founded
the Triple Five Group Ltd. (555), named after the 551
(plus four family members) Iranian investors who managed to sneak millions out of Iran for the Ghermezians
to invest.*

SIMON McTAVISH
1750–1840
King of the Hills and Thrills

Almost completely unknown to modern-day Canadians, Simon McTavish was the man to see in mid-18th-century Canada if you wished to survive in the wilds. McTavish imported products such as rum, wine, iron, guns and gunpowder, and he contracted with area farmers for wheat flour and with First Nation tribes for huge supplies of lyed corn, known as "Indian meal." He also arranged with First Nation tribes for the construction of special canoes to ship his goods into the wilderness. In went his supplies and out came his furs, first to his trading post at Detroit, and after the Revolutionary War began in 1774, to Montréal, where he threw in with the Frobisher brothers and 20 other investors to form the North West Company.

McTavish liked to drink, fight and mingle with his voyageurs, and from 1775 until his demise in 1804, he was the virtual ruler of Canada West, controlling much of Rupert's Land and even emulating the HBC in minting his own beaver buck currency. If there was money around, Simon McTavish was there to make it; he owned sawmills, banks, lumberyards, barrel factories and even a company that baked cookies. No prissy Londoner, he was a Scotsman and knew the value of a dollar, and over time, he became the richest man in Canada. However, he was no stranger to having fun, and one of his favourite winter pastimes was tobogganing down a hill on Montréal's Mount Royal. He liked tobogganing so much that he chose his preferred sledding spot as the site on which to build Canada's first castle.

Montréal's richest man, McTavish fell ill and died in 1804 at the age of 54. Although he passed away before his mansion was completed, he was buried on that toboggan slope, and for years afterward, his ghost was seen sliding down that hill in his coffin in winter, laughing and having a good old time. The ghost of Simon McTavish was spotted by so many Montréalers that in 1861, the city tore down his castle and covered over his mausoleum. This was done ostensibly to keep away grave robbers, but the reality had more to do with the happy, toboggan-riding spook that was depreciating property values on ritzy Mount Royal. In 2010, archaeologists uncovered McTavish's mausoleum, and today, the fun-loving ghost is back and making Mount Royal a favourite venue of Montréal spook tours.

DID YOU KNOW?

The brass token was a common form of currency in Canada, and though British sterling was the official currency, tokens were issued by all manner of businesses right into the 20th century. Banks, general stores, livery stables, taverns and mining and lumber companies all issued tokens that were as good as gold.

The most common token used during Canada's formative years was the brass "beaver buck," a rather large coin issued by the Hudson's Bay Company. Each coin had a hole drilled through the top so that they could be conveniently strung together and worn around the neck since pockets in clothing were a rarity. One token was equal in value to a single beaver pelt and could be redeemed for merchandise at any Hudson's Bay trading post.

TIMOTHY EATON
1834–1907
He Threw a Mean Snowball

Born in Northern Ireland two months after his father passed away, Timothy Eaton, along with his four brothers and three sisters, was raised by his mother and enjoyed a reasonably comfortable life until it was interrupted by the potato famine of 1846. While two of his brothers and all three sisters immigrated to Canada, Timothy stayed behind to look after his mother.

Timothy withdrew from school and apprenticed himself to a Mister Smith, a distant cousin and the owner of a small grocery store, and began to learn a trade. His apprenticeship completed in 1852, Timothy went to work at another store for a year, garnering more experience and enough money to follow his siblings to Canada in 1854 and into the history books.

In 1869, Timothy moved from Kirkton, Ontario, to Toronto, where he set up a store on Yonge Street. Using careful thought, innovation and Methodist contacts, Timothy Eaton rose to the very apex of retail stardom and showed the world how to sell stuff. Cash on the barrelhead was not his innovation, but "money back if not satisfied" was, and as he moved up the ladder of success, he added more innovations, such as free gift-wrapping and delivery.

Deeply religious, a teetotaller and a nose-to-the-grindstone guy, Timothy could still get himself embroiled in snowball fights with his always-nearby competitor, Robert Simpson. In 1882, in a bid to shake free of Simpson, Timothy bought property on Trinity Square in downtown Toronto, and by 1884, he had erected a brand-new store of epic proportions. He kept the lease on the old location to keep Simpson from moving in, but his competitor followed him, erecting a store of almost equally epic proportions right next to Timothy's. More snowball fights ensued, as well as many more innovations, such as a catalogue in 1884, waiting rooms, sale days and free bus rides, all designed to keep customers in Timothy's store and not Simpson's.

By the early 20th century, the T. Eaton Company and its ready-to-wear clothing factories sprawled over 22 acres (9 hectares) of downtown Toronto, with direct buying offices in major European cities, making Timothy Eaton Canada's champion snowball thrower.

ELIZABETH ARDEN
1884–1966
Make It Big and Red, and Change My Name

In 1908, Florence Nightingale Graham escaped a menial shopkeeper's future in Woodbridge, Ontario, by taking her brother's offer of a spare room in his house in New York

City. Florence had little education, but she landed a job as a bookkeeper at the E.R. Squibb Pharmaceutical Company. While there, she spent hours learning about skincare in the company's lab, and then, with her new-found skills, went to work for Eleanor Adair, an early beauty culturist, giving facials and other beauty treatments.

Quick to learn, Florence and her friend Elizabeth opened their own facial shop the next year on New York's fashionable Fifth Avenue. Less than a year later, her friend had departed, leaving Florence on her own. She needed to remove Elizabeth's name from the gold-leaf sign above the door, but as she was standing outside watching the sign workers, Florence had an epiphany and decided to change her name. She told the workers to remove her name, leave the first name of her partner and add another to it, that of Arden, from her favourite Tennyson poem, "Enoch Arden." As an afterthought, she gave the work-men instructions that would create an icon in the cosmetics industry, "Change the door. Make it big, paint it red and put a big, brass nameplate smack in the middle. Oh, and make the sign read Elizabeth Arden Salons."

The Elizabeth Arden line of cosmetics would become hugely successful, but Elizabeth's love life suffered, with all three of her marriages ending in divorce. But no problem, as Elizabeth found another love, horse racing, and in 1947, almost 70 years old but looking 40, Elizabeth Arden was in the stands at Churchill Downs to watch her horse Jet Pilot win the Kentucky Derby.

JACOB GHERMEZIAN
1902–2000
Our King of the Shopping Malls

Born in Azerbaijan and brought up in Tehran, Iran, Jacob Ghermezian was not happy in the family carpet business and longed to build something visionary. That vision was a gated community with apartments, stores, restaurants and recreation facilities. Completed during the early 1920s, the Ghermezian complex was such a success that it ingrained itself into Jacob's psyche. Forced to sell out and leave Tehran during the early 1940s, Jacob returned to selling carpets, first in New York City, then in Montréal, and by 1964, he had 16 retail stores across the U.S. and Canada.

Ever the visionary, Ghermezian moved to Edmonton, Alberta, in 1967 and began investing in real estate with an eye to recreating his Tehran complex. He thought that if it worked there, it should work in Edmonton, and with his four sons on board, his vision might become reality if he could just raise the capital. In 1979, Ghermezian got a break when the Alberta government purchased a section of land that he had cobbled together for a housing development, giving him an $18-million profit that he used to begin reconstructing a much grander version of his Tehran complex—West Edmonton Mall.

FRANK GEHRY
1929–

Splendour in the Glass

Frank Gehry was born Ephraim Owen Goldberg on February 28, 1929, at his grandparents' house in Toronto at 15 Beverly Street, near his first Canadian architectural undertaking—the redesign of the Art Gallery of Ontario. In 1947,

Frank and his parents moved to Los Angeles, where his father changed the family's name to Gehry before they applied for U.S. citizenship. Frank adopted his new first name a few years later.

Enrolled at LA City College, Frank took an architectural course as an incidental but soon became so enthralled by the subject that he managed to earn a scholarship to the University of Southern California, from which he graduated with a degree in architecture in 1954. For the next eight years, Frank bounced around; he worked for several firms, got married, took courses, did a stint in the army, had two kids and spent a year working in Paris before returning to Los Angeles in 1964 to open his own firm, Gehry Associates. For a number of years, Frank designed conventional buildings, but by the end of the 1970s, he was moving away from the conventional into more imaginative designs, with projects such as the California Aerospace Museum and the Loyola University Law School building.

During the 1980s, Frank concentrated on designing for international clients, and in 1989, he received the Pritzker Architecture Prize, the highest award in architecture. In 1990,

Frank's design for the Weisman Art Museum at the University of Minnesota (see photo opposite) launched him into architectural stardom, especially after completion of his Guggenheim Museums in Bilbao, Spain, and Abu Dhabi, United Arab Emirates, and his tour de force Walt Disney Concert Hall in downtown L.A.

Along the path to stardom, Frank also created designs for watches, furniture, liquor bottles and the World Cup of Hockey trophy. Frank Gehry is an architect for all seasons, and in what he described as an emotional experience, he returned home in 2004 to give Torontonians a fusion of light, wood and his wonderful imagination in the newly renovated Art Gallery of Ontario.

DID YOU KNOW?

In 1926, Guelph, Ontario, expat J. Frank Grimes led a group of investors that opened America's first Independent Grocers Alliance (IGA) food market in Chicago, Illinois. Toronto resident Ray Wolfe, owner of the Oshawa Wholesale Group, obtained the first IGA franchise for Canada in 1951, and by 1997, Oshawa Wholesale was servicing over 500 stores.

In 1998, supermarket giant Sobeys of the Maritimes purchased the Oshawa Wholesale Group and opened their first store outside the Atlantic provinces in Guelph, adding credence to the saying, "What goes around, comes around."

The Politicos

They arrived as immigrants and stayed to help build a nation. Although the first politicians were usually younger sons of the British aristocracy appointed to rubber stamp the edicts passed by British military governors, they were soon replaced by elected legislators with a keener interest in nation building. More than a few were also keen on feathering their own nests, with corruption becoming the business of politics, and when it came to great projects such as bridges, roads, railways and lumbering concessions, the hands of Canadian politicos were outstretched like the branches of a maple tree. The times were weird, wild and wonderful, and, corruption aside, the end product was nothing less than magical.

SIR JOHN ALEXANDER MACDONALD
1815–91
Our King of Cups

In 1872, Prime Minister John A. Macdonald rose in the House of Commons to address members who were howling for his resignation over a perceived botched treaty with the U.S. In a calm voice, he informed his colleagues that, because of his secret negotiations while a member of the Washington Treaty Commission, Canada would receive millions from the Americans as compensation for the Fenian raids of 1866 to 1871, along with an agreement from the British guaranteeing loans for the construction of the Canadian Pacific Railway. It was a political *fait accompli*, made possible by the fraternal order of Freemasons, since all the members of the Washington Treaty belonged to that brotherhood and were

obliged to help fellow Freemason John A. Macdonald cement his place in Canadian politics.

Place is something that Sir John would drink to, along with anything else, as alcoholic benders were his favourite pastime, much to the delight of his political arch-enemy George Brown of the *Toronto Globe*, who published "sick notices" in his paper whenever the prime minister got into his cups, which was often. In 1873, Macdonald's government resigned and lost the 1874 election because Sir John accepted illegal campaign contributions from shipping magnate Sir Hugh Allan in the infamous Pacific Scandal, an episode that many historians blame on Sir John's heavy drinking. Macdonald denied any impropriety in the affair, even after a telegram from him demanding another $10,000 from Allan was made public. Sir John's second wife, Susan Agnes, could not stand his drinking bouts, and while forced to accompany her husband on a cross-country train trip in 1886, vacated the train and installed herself as far from him as possible—on the locomotive's cowcatcher.

AMOR DE COSMOS
1825–97
Truth, Justice and the Canadian Way

During the 19th century, the weird and wonderful gravitated to the West Coast like bees to honey. Gold was the honey, and in 1853, it lured William Alexander Smith from a secure mercantile job in Halifax to Placerville, California, not to grub for gold, but to take photographs of the grubbers. Miners lucky enough to strike it rich wanted the event memorialized, and Billy Smith was ready to oblige for a tiny share.

Tired of being Bill Smith, he petitioned the California State Assembly for a name change to "Amor De Cosmos" to denote his love of order, beauty and the universe. A little weird, but what the heck, those were strange times. In 1858, anticipating the gold rush to the Fraser River, Cosmos went north to Vancouver Island to become a building contractor at Fort Victoria and a newspaper publisher. Always interested in politics, his newspaper, the *British Colonist*, kept him in the public eye and allowed him to rail against what he called the "Family Compact" of BC, the cartel government of former HBC factor, Governor James Douglass.

Land speculator, newspaperman and growing increasingly more eccentric, De Cosmos jumped into BC politics with both feet. He advocated the amalgamation of Vancouver Island with mainland British Columbia, as well as BC's entry into Canadian Confederation, a policy that would make him a Father of Confederation. In 1872, De Cosmos became the province's second premier, but he had to resign two years later because of his eccentric behaviour and because he was feathering his own nest through insider land speculation. His idiosyncrasies included a fixation on political issues, fistfights with legislators, bursts of rage and crying in the legislature and inappropriate use of his newspaper. In 1880, in an attempt to bolster his political image for an upcoming federal election, he merged his newspaper with the *Victoria Times* to form the still-in-print *Victoria Times Colonist*, but he lost the election and retired to Victoria.

After he retired, his eccentricities blossomed to include a fear of anything electrical, outbursts of public rage and the financing of weird business ventures, such as a hot-food delivery service to miners. In 1895, Amor De Cosmos lost touch with reality completely and was declared a menace to society and confined to an insane asylum.

SIR WILLIAM MACKENZIE
1849–1923
Can You Loan Me a Few Bucks?

Born in Kirkfield, Ontario, a small village on the Talbot River just east of Lake Simcoe, William Mackenzie received an early entrepreneurial education selling railway ties to the Midland Railway. That led to his owning a local grist and sawmill and to more small rail-laying contracts, and then eventually to laying track and building bridges in western Canada for the Canadian Pacific Railway. Short of funds to fulfill his contracts for the CPR, Mackenzie returned home and, using IOUs, bought every horse and mule in the district along with an abandoned sawmill and shipped it all west.

In 1890, his contracts complete, Mackenzie arrived in Toronto a wealthy man and joined with George Kiely and others to buy the Toronto Street Railway. Some months later, Kiely resigned as president of the trolley line, and Mackenzie took over the position. He quickly turned what had been an almost bankrupt concern into a paying proposition called the Toronto Railway Company (TRC). Timber had led Mackenzie into the railway business just as the needs of his streetcars for electricity would lead him into the business of electricity. He bought the Electric Development Company, the main Niagara Falls hydro generating company, set up the Toronto Power Company to get the electricity to Toronto and created the Toronto Electric Light Company to distribute that electricity to customers. In 1885, Mackenzie rolled several suburban streetcar companies into his Electric Light Company and formed the Toronto and York Radial Railway, the city's first interurban network of electric streetcar routes.

In 1887, Mackenzie bought "Benvenuto," a magnificent mansion built by real estate developer Simeon H. James, though he spent little time there. He was always in some faraway place developing new ventures, including the Canadian Northern Railway, and new electrical systems in countries such as Brazil, where his efforts sowed the seeds of the mighty Brascan empire and got him knighted in 1911.

In 1918, Sir William lost the Canadian Northern Railway to a federal expropriation, and in the early 1920s, during what city politicians called the "Clean-up Deal," his business creations within the city were also expropriated. The city got the Toronto Railway Company, the Toronto Electric Light Company and the Toronto York Radial Railway, and Sir William received $11.5 million of taxpayers' money through an arbitration award. For Mackenzie, it was like winning the lottery—not a bad end for an entrepreneur who employed IOUs and the trust of neighbours to finance his spectacular rise to financial stardom.

WILLIAM LYON MACKENZIE KING
1874–1950
The Dog Had His Ear

Grandson of his rebel namesake, William Lyon Mackenzie, King was the longest-serving prime minister in the history of the British Commonwealth and Canada's guiding force during World War II. On the other hand, perhaps his dead dog Pat was the guiding force, as King, a firm believer in the occult, would often confer with the spirit of his pooch on matters of state. He consulted other spirits as well in séances conducted by a veritable cross-country network of spiritual mediums. That he managed to keep his spiritualist activities secret from the public was amazing—his faith in the supernatural only

became public knowledge with the release of the 30,000-page diary he kept from 1893 until his death. King wanted the diary destroyed except for certain parts that he had indicated, only he forgot to mark any of the diary. It is now available online for perusal and makes for interesting reading, especially the notes about his various dogs, all named Pat.

Spiritualism aside, King was exceptionally good at his job, so perhaps there is something to be said for consulting with the spirits of deceased canines.

WILLIAM ABERHART
1878–1943
The Bible Banger

Born in Seaforth, Ontario, William Aberhart taught school in Brantford before moving to Calgary, Alberta, in 1905, where he began teaching religion. By 1913, Aberhart's Bible classes were the largest in the province and provided him the financial security necessary for his construction of a blueprint for humanity, a chart of God's intentions for the human race.

When World War I began, Aberhart called the Kaiser "the devil personified" and would point to the spot on his chart that predicted his enemy's movements. The media called Aberhart mad, but his adherents followed him like mice after the Pied Piper, and when Canadian inventor Reginald Fessenden took the technological kinks out of radio transmissions, Aberhart broadcast his message across the province and collected money to build his Calgary Prophetic Bible Institute. In 1932, with the Great Depression gnawing at the economy, he combined the economic principles of British engineer C.H. Douglas into what he called "God's Great Economy" and created a political whirlwind called the Social Credit Party.

During the 1930s, Aberhart, dubbed "Wild Bill" by the media, turned control of Alberta's provincial government over to two members of Douglas' staff and attempted to curtail the power of the press and oust the RCMP from provincial policing duties. This was all too much for the federal government, and during an RCMP raid on the offices of the Social Credit Party, they discovered documents advocating the assassination of several Alberta bankers.

Aberhart's political career should have been finished, but the public stresses of World War I saw his party re-elected by a small majority, and his Social Credit fantasy hung on for a few more years before finally being put to rest, as was Wild Bill Aberhart, who succumbed to cirrhosis of the liver in 1943. Not exactly a wild or wonderful guy, but surely one of the weirdest in Canadian history.

CHARLOTTE WHITTEN
1896–1975
A Politico with Chutzpah

Ottawa-born Charlotte Whitten was a crackerjack athlete, and at Queen's University, she excelled not only in many athletic endeavours, but also as a journalist on the school's paper, becoming its first female editor. Soon after graduation, Charlotte jumped into socio-politics by forming the Canadian Council on Child Welfare and becoming a drumbeater for women's rights. In 1938, she helped form the Canadian National Committee on Refugees, earning the enmity of Jewish organizations for her part in blocking the wholesale import of refugees, with a few branding her anti-Semitic.

Whitten was not anti-Semitic; she was a consummate anglophile and only wanted to maintain Canada's British heritage and traditions, a fact later attested to when she fought tooth and nail to keep Prime Minister Lester Pearson from changing the Red Ensign to the newly proposed flag, the Pearson Pennant, which she called "a white badge of surrender with three dying maple leaves."

In 1951, Grenville Goodwin, the mayor of Ottawa, died and Whitten was appointed to the position, a job she took to like a fish to water. She ran the Ottawa city council with a mixture of expertise and volatile wit that became legendary, especially her statement that "Whatever women do they must do twice as well as men to be thought half as good. Luckily, this is not difficult."

Whitten never married but carried on a long relationship with her constant companion and housemate, Margaret Grier, a woman that Whitten had known and loved since her college days.

JACQUES FERRON
1921–85
He Lived Life on the Edge

Louisville, Québec, native Jacques Ferron served as a medic during World War II and became a physician after his tour was over. In 1948, he moved to Longueuil, Québec, where he authored a play, *L'Ogre*, the following year. Forced to leave town after being denounced as a communist by the local priest, Ferron moved to Montréal, where he balanced his medical practice with writing short stories, dramas, poetry and a collection of politically leaning fables called *Contes du pays incertain*, which earned him recognition as an author along with a Governor General's Award.

Ever the political satirist, Ferron founded a political party in 1963 called the Rhinoceros Party of Canada, with

a platform that promised to keep none of its promises.
In 1969, he joined the Parti Québécois and underwent therapy
for suicidal tendencies several times. During the October
Crisis of 1970, Ferron acted as a go-between with the separat-
ists, wrote a few more uninspired novels and finally fell victim
to his suicidal tendencies in 1985.

MARTIN BRIAN MULRONEY
1939–
I Can Fix That, No Problem

Brian Mulroney is from Baie-Comeau, an isolated paper-mill
town in Québec's extreme east, a place where people speak
both English and French and the only way out of town for an
intelligent young man is to pursue an education. Mulroney's
road led to St. Francis Xavier University in Antigonish, Nova
Scotia, where he became involved in politics and learned public speaking and the art of cultivating friends destined for high
places, an action commonly known as "brown nosing." Not
much of a student, Mulroney nevertheless managed to get into
Dalhousie Law School but flunked out his first year and tried
again at Laval University in Québec City. There he discovered
a goldmine of good-to-know people, including student president Joe Clark.

After graduation, Mulroney articled with the Montréal law
firm of Ogilvy Renault, where he had to fall back on his
brown-nosing expertise because he flunked his bar exams
twice. When he finally did pass, he practised as a labour lawyer until 1974, when he took an expensive run at being leader
of the Conservative Party after Robert Stanfield's resignation.
He failed and it cost him over $500,000.

Mulroney needed money badly, and the Iron Ore Company of
Canada (IOC) needed a front man with political connections,

so he was hired on as executive vice-president. In 1978, the IOC made him president and the bucks rolled in, especially after he learned to sell the company's shares en bloc to foreign concerns. In 1983, a year before the federal election, he ran against his old pal Joe Clark for leadership of the PCs and won, but lost the 1984 election to short-term Liberal prime minister John Turner, who, wanting a majority government, called for another election in September.

John Turner was a handsome man, but in the candidates' debate, Mulroney clobbered him over the issue of Trudeau's patronage appointments and froze him speechless. Mulroney and his PCs won 211 seats, the most ever, and he rose to the pulpit of power like Superman. However, the pulpit must have contained kryptonite because the public slowly became aware that Brian Mulroney was mortal with few political talents except those of making expensive accords that never flew, selling off Crown corporations and brown nosing high-ranking American politicians.

By 1992, Mulroney's Gallup poll approval rating had slumped to 11 percent, making him the most unpopular prime minister in Canadian history. The following year, in a move to set up Kim Campbell to be the fall girl for the election disaster, he resigned. It was hardly the end of an era, though, because the guy is always in the newspapers and is back with his old firm Ogilvy Renault, representing international firms in need of expert political brown nosing.

AVRIL PHAEDRA DOUGLAS "KIM" CAMPBELL
1947–
A Big Noise from a Small Town

Born in Port Alberni, British Columbia, Kim Campbell reminded people of a cartoon character, with her feet flying and ready to flash into the big time. For Kim, the big time was politics, and she climbed the ladder of success to the top one rung at a time, with a sharp eye for opportunity. In 1984, she ran for a seat in the BC legislature and lost, but picked up a job as policy advisor to Social Credit Premier Bill Bennett. Two years later, she won a seat in the legislature.

In 1988, she jumped several rungs of the ladder by winning in the federal riding vacated by MP Pat Carney, and in 1990, she became Canada's first female Minister of Justice. Three years

later, she was nearly at the top of the ladder looking down into the abyss as Minister of National Defence, the job just below the rung of prime minister, which was occupied at the time by Brian Mulroney. She should have smelled a rat but was so busy grasping at opportunity that she fell for the setup hook, line and sinker.

Brian Mulroney resigned and Kim took over as prime minister, inheriting such a political mess that it almost spelled the end of the Conservative Party. Prime Minister Kim fell off the ladder big time but eventually found her way into a place with even more opportunities, the U.S., where she's climbing a different ladder, beginning with a teaching post at Harvard University.

PENNY ELAINE HOAR
1952–97
A Rose Is a Rose Is a Rose

Toronto native Penny Hoar is best remembered for her two election runs as a member of the Rhinoceros Party on a safe-sex platform that included a free condom attached to her giveaway literature. A one-time model, artist, world traveller and general *bon vivant*, Penny's specialty was teaching transvestites and cross-dressers how to be more feminine.

Penny was the prostitutes' champion, and as a member of the Sex Workers Alliance of Toronto and a director of Maggie's, the Toronto Prostitutes Community Service Project, she worked tirelessly for the benefit of Toronto hookers. Although a bit short on decorum, Penny Hoar was a weird, wild and wonderful Canadian with a big heart.

Our Pirates
and Smugglers

*Most people have little or no understanding of the who,
what and why of those individuals who were in the
business of taking other people's property on the high
seas for financial gain, those folks commonly referred to
as "pirates." Historians like to portray pirates as cut-
throat brigands with no flag but the infamous skull and
bones, and though a few nasty characters did ply the
waves in that manner, most were businessmen or privateers financed by large investment or trading companies
with a Royal Commission that allowed them to loot
and pillage as long as they shared with the Crown.*

*England's Queen Elizabeth I became hooked on the
booty of privateers and wrote so many commissions,
called "letters of marque," that they became a major
reason for the formation of the Spanish Armada and its
odious mission to overthrow Elizabeth and put an end
to English privateering. The Armada's failure spurred*

Elizabeth to write even more commissions as a way of punishing Spain and enriching the English treasury in the process. Her successor, Charles I, attempted to appease the Spanish, French and Dutch by outlawing privateering, but he only succeeded in bankrupting his treasury and inflaming the Protestant-controlled Parliament into a civil war that cost him his head. His successor, Oliver Cromwell, immediately reinstated privateer commissions and created a virtual pirate navy to plunder the seas from Newfoundland to the Caribbean.

While the "golden age" of piracy occurred between 1690 and 1740, Newfoundland remained the private preserve of merchant traders, who were not shy about engaging in piracy and smuggling and who continued their activities well into the 20th century. In the early days, Newfoundland's privateers were mostly solo French or English naval deserters with a penchant for grabbing what they could while they could, wrecking ships with cannon shot, seizing cargos and leaving no survivors to tell tales. However, clearer heads soon realized that ships were often more valuable than their cargos, with both privateers and pirates terrorizing their quarry into surrendering undamaged craft.

Privateering went hand in hand with smuggling, as the privateers were simply opportunistic merchants

who were not averse to cheating the King's customs collector of his due. Canadian merchant ships returning from the Caribbean with cargos of sugar and molasses would routinely stop off at Boston to exchange a portion of their cargo for distilled spirits, tea and cloth, which they would offload at some deserted beach near their homeport.

During the War of 1812, flour that sold for $12 per hundredweight in the Maritimes could be purchased in the U.S. for $3, and anyone with a small boat was in business. Buying smuggled goods became so ingrained into life in the Maritime provinces that it followed westward expansion, with owners of general stores often stocking half their shelves with goods smuggled from the U.S. It was a game of sorts and was played big time during the 20th century, when smugglers changed direction and carried millions of bottles of liquor from Canada into the U.S.

CAPTAIN PETER EASTON
1570–162?
The "Notorious Pirate Admiral"

Of all the colourful characters that sailed the bounding main to pillage and loot, none was more successful or so overlooked by historians as the Englishman Peter Easton. Philip II of Spain's mighty Armada had come a cropper in 1588, and Queen Elizabeth I had decreed a time of punishment for Spain and sent out dozens of privateers with orders to plunder anything that looked remotely Spanish. To one of her young captains, Peter Easton, she assigned the task of protecting English merchant concerns in the New World fishing grounds and plundering interlopers.

Easton was the Queen's man through and through, but in 1603, Elizabeth died and James I took over the throne, made peace with the Spanish and stopped supplying English privateers. Left high and dry in Newfoundland, Easton decided that he was not the king's man and turned to piracy. He was more politician than plunderer and most always eschewed combat for a good palaver to convince opponents that breathing was better than a ball in the gut. This technique worked so well that he soon had a fleet of 10 ships with dedicated crews that pillaged the high seas from the Spanish Main to the Mediterranean Sea.

Easton at first headquartered his fleet at Harbour Grace on Newfoundland's Avalon Peninsula and later at Ferryland, a fortified position unassailable from land or sea and protected by over 100 captured cannons. From there, Easton successfully fought off a French expedition that tried to crush his hold on Newfoundland. In 1610, with his flotilla now numbering nearly 40 ships, Easton managed to blockade the Bristol Channel, demanding a "protection" toll from every ship using

England's western ports. What could the English do but pay? Easton, who now carried the title of "Notorious Pirate Admiral," had faster ships, more cannons and better sailors than the English navy.

Captain Peter Easton was a force to be avoided, so the English decided to take him out by the roots. They sent a flotilla to Newfoundland to deprive the Notorious Pirate Admiral of his home base, but Easton caught them in St. John's Harbour and took most of their ships as prizes along with local cod merchant, author and noted jurist, Sir Richard Whitbourne. Easton kept Whitbourne a prisoner on board his ship for weeks and tried to convince the jurist to join his pirate fraternity, an invitation Whitbourne steadfastly refused, though he eventually agreed to travel back to England to try to acquire a pardon for Easton. James I agreed, but the pardon never reached Easton.

Tired of waiting for Whitbourne, who thought the pirate admiral had already received his pardon, Captain Easton, who by now commanded a fleet of almost 50 ships, set sail for the Caribbean, where he captured the mighty fort of El Morro Castle in Puerto Rico along with a Spanish galleon loaded stem to stern with gold. Back at Harbour Grace, he found his base plundered by a new pirate, Henry Mainwaring, and with no word from Whitbourne, Easton sailed to the Mediterranean in 1614, where he established himself on the Barbary Coast and collaborated with the king of Algiers to raid Spanish shipping.

Some time around 1617, Captain Easton disbanded his fleet, bought a palace at Ville Franche in the pirate kingdom of Savoy and retired with a fortune so large that it enabled him to marry into nobility and acquire the title of Marquis of Savoy. Captain Peter Easton, Canada's king of pirates and the inspiration for every Hollywood swashbuckler movie ever made, lived life to the fullest and died a rich, happy man.

DID YOU KNOW?

Privateers of old flew under the flag of their nation, with the British privateer flag being the "Red Jack," an oversized Union Jack on a red background. True pirates who owed allegiance to no country flew the "Black Jack," a solid-black flag sometimes embellished with a white skull and crossed swords or bones.

SIR HENRY MAINWARING
1586–1653
The Gentleman Pirate

Henry Mainwaring derived from good English stock—his maternal grandfather was Sir William More, Vice-Admiral of Sussex—and as such, Mainwaring was privy to a fine education at Oxford. After graduation, he practised law, served as an officer in the Low Country expeditions of King James I and spent time at sea.

Mainwaring was an excellent sailor and his "all sheets to the wind" style caught the attention of his boss, Lord High Admiral Charles Howard, the 1st Earl of Nottingham, who assigned him a special task—to find, capture or kill the Notorious Pirate Admiral, Peter Easton.

Easton had accumulated a fleet of about 40 ships and had taken to stationing some in the Bristol Channel to collect safe-passage tolls from merchantmen, and Bristol traders had demanded that something be done. Mainwaring took his commission to mean something else entirely, as no one in their right mind would go after the pirate Easton with a single ship, even one as well armed and as fast as the *Resistance*, a 160-tonne, narrow-beamed corsair purchased by Mainwaring himself.

In 1610, as an official king's privateer with a letter of marque, Captain Mainwaring sailed off to do his boss proud. He didn't go anywhere near the pirate Peter Easton, though, but sailed instead to the Mediterranean's Barbary Coast to be closer to Spain. Within the year, operating from the town of Manora, Mainwaring had captured and plundered over 30 Spanish merchantmen and returned to England with so much loot that the king rewarded him with land and a castle.

The following year, the Lord High Admiral once again commissioned Mainwaring to go after Easton and this time provided him with five ships of the line. Mainwaring set sail for Easton's domain, the New World island now called Newfoundland, and arrived there with eight ships—his fleet somehow grew, either through piracy or by voluntary enlistment.

Captain Mainwaring found Easton's homeport of Harbour Grace abandoned, as the arch-pirate had sailed to the Caribbean to attack the Spanish at Puerto Rico. Mainwaring moved right in and conscripted some 400 men, as well as ordnance and victuals, from every ship and coastal settlement. For three years, Mainwaring plundered Basque, Portuguese and French ships, becoming another pirate admiral with a price on his head.

In 1614, his holds stuffed with loot, Captain Mainwaring and his private fleet of eight ships and 500 men returned to England, threw themselves on the mercy of King James I and received pardons in exchange for most of their booty and promises to give up their piratical ways. In 1618, private citizen Henry Mainwaring encountered a fleet of Newfoundland-bound ships captured by pirates while on a sailing voyage to visit relatives at Dover. Having been something of a pirate himself, Mainwaring knew how to talk to his attackers and succeeded in having his ships released. For his bravado, he was knighted Sir Henry Mainwaring and, taking advantage of his popularity, ran for and won a seat in Parliament.

King Charles I appointed Mainwaring a vice-admiral in 1639, but what should have been an "all's well that ends well" was not to be, as Sir Henry chose to fight for Charles I in the English Civil War against Oliver Cromwell. Having been on the losing side of the conflict, Sir Henry was exiled to the island of Jersey, where he died with little but his Canadian swashbuckling memories for company.

JOHN BARTHOLOMEW "BLACK BART" ROBERTS
1682–1722
The Evil Pirate

In 1714, the War of Spanish Succession ended, and, no longer needing a large navy, England mothballed or sold off two-thirds of its ships, cut manpower from 54,000 to 6000 and cancelled all letters of marque to privateers. Bartholomew Roberts, a young Royal Navy sailor, found himself out of a job and was forced to take unsatisfactory positions aboard various unsatisfactory ships.

In 1722, while Roberts was serving as third mate aboard a slaver, the pirate Howell Davis seized the ship. Forced to join Davis' crew, Roberts decided that his new motto would be to live a short and merry life, and he completely embraced the life of a pirate. A few months later, during an ambush by Portuguese pirates, Captain Howell was shot dead and Roberts was elected captain because of his navigational skills. His first order was to destroy the Portuguese who had killed his captain. That done, he sailed off to scour the Caribbean, capturing many ships before sailing to Newfoundland, where he ravaged the coastal settlements, taking men and supplies and a few French merchantmen, one of a size that made for a perfect pirate vessel.

Roberts always dressed like a London gentleman in a red velvet waistcoat draped with a brace of pistols and topped off by large, feathered hat. He also designed his own black pirate flag, complete with a picture of him brandishing a cutlass and standing on two skulls. If that wasn't terrifying enough, he press-ganged musicians to play for his crew and had them beat drums whenever the ship went on the attack.

In 1720, Roberts sailed into Trepassey, Newfoundland, with drums beating and cannons firing, and succeeded in terrorizing the town and the captains of 18 ships into surrendering. He was there for weeks refitting his ships, and he paid in gold for all the work and everything he took, which goes a long way to explaining why the residents of Trepassey never sent for help.

Roberts was a religious man, but in spite of that, he began to display a cruel streak that ran hot and cold—he was just as likely to slaughter a ship's crew as he was to set them free. His pirate career ended in the fall of 1722, when under attack by two British naval ships, he leapt onto a gun carriage to direct fire, only to have his throat ripped out by grapeshot. Live by the gun, die by the gun.

As a pirate, Roberts was immensely successful, capturing over 400 ships, with 55 taken off the Newfoundland coast. But what happened to the considerable treasure from all those ships? After Robert's death, his crew lost their will to fight and surrendered to British attackers—two ships, captained by two men named Ogle and Hill. Captain Ogle admitted to finding two treasures, one small and one huge, but when the time came to transfer the large treasure to his ship, it had somehow disappeared, along with Captain Hill's vessel. That those two ships should return to England at about the same time with only the small treasure aboard suggests that both captains probably retired from the sea in some comfort.

SAMUEL "SAM" BRONFMAN
1889–1971
The King of Swig

"Bronfman" means "liquor man" in Yiddish, and when the U.S. passed the National Prohibition Act in 1919, Canadian brothers Sam and Harry Bronfman decided to become big-time liquor men, a term they made synonymous with smuggling. The Bronfmans, however, never broke a Canadian or Ontario prohibition law because, even though prohibition existed in Canada, the manufacturing of spirits was never

actually banned. Distilleries were allowed to make and bottle whisky, but it had to be sold outside the country.

When word that two Jewish brothers from Canada were making top-quality hooch in Montréal, Meyer Lansky, a kingpin in New York City's Jewish mafia, told Sam Bronfman, "We'll take all the booze you can ship. All you gotta do is get it over the border. We'll take it from there." Sam Bronfman only had to fill up a ship, make the declaration to customs that the whisky was destined for Europe or South America and then send the ship across the St. Lawrence River.

Ever the salesman, Sam began cultivating new American customers such as Arnold Rothstein, "Waxy" Gordon, "Big Maxie" Greenberg and a host of other East Coast mob bosses. Bronfman whisky fuelled booze cans, created Mafia families from their more ambitious operators and gave rise to money laundering.

After a few years of this, the U.S. got serious about the prohibiting the sale and consumption of liquor, so when the St. Lawrence River became too hot for smuggling, Sam looked to Lake Erie. It was a much safer channel, but its best area, the Detroit River, had already been staked out by the Bronfmans' main competition, Seagram Company Ltd. (whose best U.S. customer was Chicago mob boss Al Capone). Not wanting to create friction with Capone, Sam and Rothstein bought isolated properties in Maine where they could unload their ships and effectively avoid U.S. customs. Their venture was successful and demand grew, as did the desire for shipments to come in faster. "More, send more," was the call from the mobsters, and Sam once again looked to Lake Erie. Small, fast speedboats could get across the lake in less than an hour, but that meant that the Bronfmans would be breaking the law, something they were loath to do, so while they were happy to supply the liquor, they left the actual transportation to others.

The speedboats would have to come from the American side but were only going to be able travel halfway across the lake, so as not to cross the border. Fishermen were the solution, because if Sam could get them to take his shipments across on the Canadian side, the Americans could pick them up in their speedboats in the middle of the lake.

Six months later, Sam's fishermen friends were operating a flotilla of fishing boats, and Sam was shipping them whisky packed in burlap bags rather than crates. There were 50 bottles to a bag, and each bag was attached to a float. The bags came by railcar, right from the distillery to the docks, and so many arrived at the lake's ports that locals began calling Lake Erie the "Jewish Lake."

From 1927 until the Prohibition Act's repeal in 1933, Sam Bronfman shipped millions of bottles of whisky to the mobs, with about 85 percent smuggled across the river to Arnold Rothstein's hometown of Detroit. The remainder made the Lake Erie trip in the boats of the midnight herring fishermen.

HAROLD CLIFFORD "HARRY" HATCH
1884–1946
He Kept the 1920s Roaring

Moving what the law deemed unmovable was a Harry Hatch specialty. When the Ontario government closed down liquor stores in 1916 to facilitate the war effort, Harry obediently shuttered his small liquor store in Whitby, Ontario, and moved to Québec to sell booze by mail order. In Québec, he discovered a loophole in Ontario law that put him on the road to riches.

Ontario's prohibition allowed the medicinal use of liquor when prescribed by a physician, and through Harry, liquor merchants and doctors would meet at soda fountains. Within two years, Harry had convinced almost every pharmacist in Ontario to build a soda fountain and even recruited underpaid physicians, some of whom simply sat beside the pharmacy door and wrote out prescriptions for Harry's hooch. In 1926, with Harry's physicians writing almost half a million prescriptions annually, the Ontario government caved in and repealed prohibition, not that Harry noticed, for he had made enough money to buy the giant distiller Gooderham and Worts and was busily moving the unmovable into the still dry-as-a-bone U.S.

In 1927, Harry bought the Hiram Walker distillery in Walkerville, Ontario, to be nearer to his major U.S. customer, Chicago gang boss Al Capone. After prohibition, Hatch bought controlling interest of Corby's as well as the Scottish distiller George Ballantine & Son, and concentrated on selling Scotch whisky and his famous Canadian Club brand on a legitimate basis. He soon became bored, so he turned to what he loved best, raising and racing thoroughbred horses, an endeavour he dominated during the 1930s and '40s. Slick as a whistle, smooth as silk and the greatest smuggler of them all, Harry C. Hatch was the weird and wonderful guy who put Canadian whisky on the world map.

JESSE WILLMS
1978–
Our Likeable Internet Pirate

An Edmonton, Alberta, homeboy, Jesse Willms has been making money and friends since he launched his first Internet business in 1994. Since then, he has created dozens of companies, selling items as diverse as weight-loss pills and teeth-whitening pens for which his boyish smile is the incentive to buy.

Jesse has made lots of money—according to the U.S. Federal Trade Commission (FTC), almost $467 million since 2007—and he likes to spread that money around to various Edmonton charities. Not much, though, just a little here and there to establish himself as a philanthropist. For this, Jesse has become a bit of celebrity in Edmonton, and not a few people were shocked to find their homeboy hero the subject of a lawsuit by the FTC on May 19, 2011, a suit that claimed Jesse was an Internet pirate employing deceptive trade practices. Apparently, customers who bought his products on a no-risk, trial basis found themselves very much at risk when large orders for pills and teeth whiteners begin arriving already charged to their credit cards.

Becoming successful at such a young age is admirable, and it is most unfortunate for both Jesse and Canada that his first lessons in business ethics will be taught by U.S. Federal Trade Commission lawyers.

The
Entertainers

The castle hotels that William Van Horne constructed for the Canadian Pacific Railway required more than fine rooms, excellent service, outstanding cuisine and fantastic vistas to keep patrons happy—they needed lots of talent to keep guests entertained when the sun went down. World famous singers, musicians, stage actors and a host of variety performers all appeared at some time or other at CP hotels or on cruise ships. Van Horne's railway and hotels turned Canada into a prime tourist destination and a major venue for the world's entertainers. However, there were many other venues for talented performers, including Niagara Falls, country fairs, variety theatres, lake cruises and any place that people gathered, which in the later part of the 19th century included the grand entertainment parks.

WILLIAM LEONARD HUNT, THE GREAT FARINI
1838–1929
Our Man on the High Wire

In 1852, Port Hope, Ontario, was a circuit stop for Pentland's Dramatic Equestrian Establishment, a classic big-top extravaganza with animals, clowns and lots of acrobats, one of whom did a wire-walking act that galvanized 14-year-old Billy Hunt. It was not long before Billy had his own wire, a rope strung between the family home and the barn, and soon he was not only emulating the circus performer but doing a better job of it. A natural-born athlete, Billy took to the high wire like a fly to sticky paper, and the following year, the town fathers invited him to try crossing the Ganaraska River, a feat he performed under the adopted name Farini with plenty of flair, including doing a somersault and hanging by his heels.

The people of Port Hope were flabbergasted by the homeboy's talent, and Billy's fame spread until he was a regular performer at travelling circuses and agricultural events. In 1860, the 22-year-old decided that the world was his oyster and boarded a train to Niagara Falls, where he announced to reporters that he, as the Great Farini, had arrived to challenge the Great Blondin for wire-walking supremacy. The battle of the wire walkers was on, and while Blondin chose to walk a narrow section of the Niagara Gorge, the Great Farini walked a slack rope almost in the spray of the mighty falls. The Great Farini bested Blondin at every turn—one of Blondin's tricks was to carry out a small stove and cook his breakfast, so Billy carried out a washing machine and did his laundry. When Blondin thought to lower cooked eggs to the *Maid of the Mist* tour boat, Billy lowered himself down to the vessel, where he enjoyed a glass of wine before climbing back to his high wire.

A financial depression forced the Great Farini to abandon the next year's lucrative antics at Niagara Falls, and he headed instead for Cuba, where during a bullring crossing, he lost his new wife when she fell from the high wire and died. In 1864, Billy joined P.T. Barnum in New York City and unsuccessfully attempted to walk across Niagara Falls on stilts, and in 1866, he toured Europe as the "Flying Farinis," a trapeze act that featured a small boy called El Niño doing death-defying trapeze leaps in front of sell-out crowds. In 1870, Billy appeared centre stage at London's Imperatrice Theatre, where he presented Lulu, a blonde, blue-eyed beauty who was in actuality El Niño, his trapeze partner, in drag. When Lulu stepped into the spotlight, she was magically catapulted to the trapeze 30 metres above the baffled and surprised spectators. Lulu's mysterious rise to the trapeze was accomplished through Billy's invention of a large spring device, a trick that would mystify audiences for years. The London act came to a crashing end in 1876, when an accident required Lulu's hospitalization and the media discovered that "she" was not female. Billy and Lulu appeared again in New York City and kept the act alive for a few years until Lulu decided to marry and move to Bridge-port, Connecticut, where he opened a photography studio that he called—what else—Farinis.

Back in England, Billy lucked out when the Royal Westminster Aquarium, a huge London entertainment com-plex, invited him to try to improve their shrinking attendance. Billy put his spring catapult invention into a mock cannon, added noise and smoke, and shot a real female partner named Zazel across the stadium floor into a net. Billy's "human can-nonball" act drove the public wild.

In 1885, Billy, along with El Niño/Lulu and the boy's father, set off into the Kalahari Desert in search of the famed Lost City of the Kalahari, which, according to him, they found, but the claim remained unsubstantiated. Billy Hunt, Canada's greatest circus showman and inventor of the famous human cannonball act would continue inventing circus contraptions from his hometown of Port Hope until the flu took him in 1929.

LOUIS CYR
1863–1912
The World's Strongest Man

Born in Saint-Cyprien-de-Napierville, Lower Canada, Louis Cyr was the second of 17 siblings but was the only one to exhibit the physical trait that would make him world famous—Louis was as strong as an ox, literally. His early years saw him employed as a lumberjack, farmer and policeman, but in 1885, he got a taste of showbiz when he was hired by Québec showman Gustave Lambert in an early version of the modern circus phenomenon, Cirque du Soleil. In 1886, Cyr took on David Michaud, the strongest man in Canada at the time, and defeated him handily, lifting 2371 pounds (1075 kilograms). Cyr could lift a platform on which stood 18 grown men and could withstand the pull of four large draft horses while holding two sets of reins in each hand. After a European tour in 1891 that garnered no challengers, he was declared the "world's strongest man," a title he held until just before he died from Bright's disease, a kidney ailment, in 1912.

ANNA HAINING BATES
1846–88
The World's Tallest Woman

Born Anna Haining Swan in Colchester County, Nova Scotia, the girl must have been something of a surprise to her parents since she weighed 18 pounds (8.2 kilograms) at birth. When she reached her full height, she stood an amazing 8 feet, 1 inch

(246 centimetres) tall and weighed almost 350 pounds (159 kilograms). A giantess, but perfectly proportioned and as smart as a whip, Anna taught Sunday school, acted in local plays and didn't mind putting herself on public display. She even put together an act, and in 1862, New York showman P.T. Barnum paid her an astronomical $1000 per month to appear at his New York museum.

In 1870, while visiting a Halifax circus, Anna met Martin Van Buren Bates, a man almost as tall as she was. She was hired by W.W. Cole, the circus owner, and Anna and Martin fell in love, married and toured as the world's tallest couple. While appearing in Europe, they were presented to Queen Victoria, who gave Anna a fine gold watch. Anna and Martin had two children, both giants, neither of which survived more than a few weeks.

ANGUS MacASKILL
1825–63
The Cape Breton Giant

Angus was already a big kid when the MacAskill family immigrated to Englishtown, Cape Breton, Nova Scotia, from Scotland in 1831. There was nothing physically abnormal about Angus, he was simply a big, perfectly proportioned young man, and when he was mature, he stood 7 feet, 9 inches (236 centimetres) tall, weighed 425 pounds (193 kilograms) and was incredibly strong. Stories that he could lift nine men caught the attention of impresario P.T. Barnum, who paid Angus a small fortune in 1849 to pair up with the tiny General Tom Thumb and go on tours that included Europe, even appearing before Queen Victoria at Buckingham Palace.

Angus loved performing feats of strength, but one would be his undoing. Taunted by a group of French sailors in New Orleans, he picked up a 2700-pound (1225-kilogram) anchor, and when he tossed it away, one of the anchor's flukes caught him in the shoulder and he sustained a crippling injury. Perhaps because of the injury, Angus quit touring and returned to Cape Breton, where he opened a general store. Ill health from his old wound sapped his strength, and he died in his bed. It was giant's bed, as was the rest of his Englishtown home, and today, its huge doorways and large rooms have been preserved as a museum that is well worth visiting.

MARY PICKFORD
1892–1979
America's Canadian Sweetheart

Born to the Smith family on April 8, 1892, "Baby" Gladys Smith would be on stage at the nearby Princess Theatre by age

five and would spend the next nine years playing Shea's Theatre in Toronto and travelling the northwestern U.S. vaudeville circuit with her manager mother, younger brother and sister. At age 15, she walked into the New York office of famous producer David Belasco and demanded a job. Belasco agreed, but only if she changed her name to Mary Pickford, and in 1907, she opened on Broadway in a Belasco play called *The Warrens of Virginia.*

In 1909, entranced by a new media called "motion pictures," Mary went to see American Biograph producer D.W. Griffith and asked for a part in a picture. She got it that afternoon and was asked to return the following day for another role, for which she would be paid $5, the same as all of Griffith's actors. But Mary told Griffith she was a Belasco actress and an artist, and demanded $10. She got her $10, but Griffith made her do a film every week, and like all Griffith actors, she got no billing. In 1910, she accompanied Griffith to California where she secretly married fellow Biograph actor Owen Moore.

The next year, Mary left Biograph and went to work for producer Carl Laemmie doing one-reelers for more money as well as star billing. Thirty-five films later, she broke her contract and returned to Biograph to do some of her best work.
In 1912, David Belasco offered Mary a part playing the little blind girl in *A Good Little Devil*, a play that fledging producer Adolph Zukor wanted to make into a film. Zukor called his film company "Famous Players in Famous Plays," the precursor to the Famous Players theatre chain.

Mary made 21 films for Zukor under his new banner "Paramount Pictures," and by 1916, she was making $150,000 per year as the most popular actress in the world. She had a new two-year contract with Zukor by the end of 1916 that had her making her own films for her own company, Pickford Films, under the Paramount umbrella, for which she received $1 million. The highlight of this venture was her production of *Rebecca of Sunnybrook Farm*.

During a campaign for war bond sales with Charlie Chaplin and Douglas Fairbanks Jr., Mary and Douglas fell in love. While they waited for their divorces to be finalized, they, along with Chaplin, formed United Artists, for which Mary made her second best grossing film, *Little Lord Fauntleroy*. She and Fairbanks were married in 1921 and lived happily for many years at their Hollywood mansion "Pickfair" until overindulgence in alcohol took a toll on them both. Their marriage ended in divorce in 1936.

Mary lived on at Pickfair, becoming the Hollywood "hostess with the mostest," and in 1937, she married actor-musician Charles "Buddy" Rogers, a relationship that endured until her death in 1979.

Perhaps Mary's most lasting legacy is the Academy of Motion Pictures, with its accompanying Oscar award, which Mary and a group of actors formed in 1928. Mary's first talking picture, *The Taming of the Shrew*, earned her the very first Oscar for the best female role.

NORMA SHEARER
1902–83
The Eyes Have It

Born in Montréal and groomed by her mother to be a professional pianist, everything changed for Norma Shearer in 1918 when her mother and father separated. Norma decided to pursue a career in films, and in 1920, Norma, her mother and her older sister, Athole, headed for New York City.

Norma was not exactly prime material for films and was rudely told so by film producer D.W. Griffith, "Your eyes are too blue, kid. On film they make you look blank, besides which they looked crossed." Norma was indeed slightly cross-eyed, and she immediately sought out a specialist, who provided her with exercises to straighten her eyes, exercises she performed daily in front of a mirror.

Needing to provide for her mother and sister, Norma took modelling jobs and was wildly successful, attracting the attention of Hollywood producer Hal Roach who, in 1923, offered her a screen test in Hollywood. The test was a disaster because the strong lights made her blue eyes look white, but when the aspiring actress was found collapsed in a hallway, the studio relented and supplied another screen test with better lighting. She landed a contract with MGM doing bit parts. Later, MGM would give her one shot at a major role in the film *Pleasure Mad*, for which she needed a lecture by studio head Louis B. Mayer to complete. Her next major role, in the film *He Who Gets Slapped*, became a box office hit for MGM, and the blue-eyed actress from Montréal was off and running to become a major Hollywood star.

RUBY KEELER
1910–96
Our Hollywood Legend

Born Ethel Hilda Keeler in Dartmouth, Nova Scotia, 13-year-old Ruby's stage career got an early boost when famous Broadway producer George Cohan placed her in the chorus line of his show, *The Rise of Rosy O'Grady*. Her rocket rise to star status began when she caught the eye of gangster Johnny Costello, who advised various Broadway producers that it would benefit their health if they gave Ruby good parts. She was only 17, and in a stage production called *Streets of New York*, she attracted the attention of that famous seducer of young girls, Al Jolson. When the pair became secretly engaged, all bets were on Jolson being rubbed out by the mob—everyone knew that Ruby was Johnny Costello's girl. On September 21, 1928, Al Jolson and Ruby Keeler were married, apparently with the blessings of Johnny Costello because the occasion was uneventful.

During Ruby's rise to film stardom, jealous Al Jolson made her life a misery until 1939, when she divorced him. Ruby did one last film before she met and married the love of her life, John Lowe. However, 30 years later, when Ruby was 61, a producer named Harry Rigby talked her and famed Hollywood director and choreographer Busby Berkeley into doing a musical stage production called *No, No, Nanette*, in which she absolutely wowed audiences.

Although she became a U.S. citizen, on visits to Canada, Ruby would always happily announce to immigration authorities that, yes, she had been born in Dartmouth. Her biographer, Howard Goodman, wrote that the Canadian-born superstar's life had been a complete success.

JACK LEONARD WARNER
1892–1978
Being Right 51 Percent of the Time Put Him Ahead of the Game

Jack Warner was born in London, Ontario, into a family of Polish immigrants who relocated to Youngstown, Ohio, when Jack was six years old. Youngstown was a tough place in those days but provided Jack a venue in which to practise his song-and-dance shtick, a talent he forgot about after seeing his first Vitaphone projection. Jack and three of his brothers, Harry, Sam and Albert, borrowed $1000, bought a second-hand

machine, rented an unused vaudeville theatre and went
into business.

In 1907, the brothers formed the Duquesne Amusement
Company to distribute independent films, a firm they sold
in 1910 for a fair chunk of cash. They used the money to support producer Carl Laemmie's Independent Motion Picture
Company in its battle against the Edison Trust and produced
their first film, *Dante's Inferno*, in 1924. Tired of fighting the
Edison film monopoly, elder brother Harry sent Jack to establish a film exchange in San Francisco and Los Angeles. Being
in LA put the brothers in the right place at the right time to
produce Warner Brothers' first major hit, *My Four Years in
Germany*, and establish a studio first in Culver City, and then
in Hollywood.

In 1927, Sam died of pneumonia a few weeks before Warner
Brothers' biggest hit, *The Jazz Singer*, with Al Jolson, began to
pump serious money into the company. Sam's death left Jack
inconsolable, and over time, he became tyrannical and heavy
handed with his stars and studio employees. His fights with
his prize contract star Jimmy Cagney were legendary and
usually ended with both men screaming obscenities at each
other in Yiddish. Although unlikable, Jack had a talent for
recognizing opportunity, and when he got a chance to enter
the talking-movie phase of motion picture production, he
jumped in with both feet.

Toward the end of the 1930s, Jack had his studio producing
antiwar movies, and during World War II, they produced
many propaganda films. After the war, Jack quarrelled even
more with his actors, and during the late 1950s, he had falling
out with his second-in-command, his son, Jack Jr., banned
him from the lot and never spoke to him again. Jack began
selling off films to competing studios for cheap, and when he
sold the cartoons, his brothers Harry and Albert complained

bitterly and threatened to sell their shares in the business. Jack said, "Fine, we'll all sell and get out." Only while his brothers were selling, Jack was secretly buying their shares to gain control of the business. After they found out what Jack was doing, his brothers never spoke to him again.

The 1960s were good for the Warner Brothers studio, but by 1969, Jack had had enough and sold his shares for real. Jack Warner passed away in 1986, but he didn't actually die outright—after suffering a stroke in 1974, he gradually faded away, like in a film shot.

DAVID VERNER
1894–1992
The Magician's Magician

Born in Ottawa, David Verner preferred New York's Coney Island as a youngster and developed a fascination for sleight-of-hand magic that would eventually earn him the nickname "The Professor." During an age when magic was the king of entertainment, Verner changed his name to "Dai Vernon" and became a master of sleight-of-hand and card tricks, but not before graduating with an engineering degree from Kingston's Royal Military College. The Great Houdini, who always claimed that if he saw a card trick three times, he could duplicate it, remained mystified even after Verner performed a trick for him seven times.

By 1924, Verner was making $5000 a month performing single-evening shows for New York's wealthiest citizens. During the 1930s, he performed in sold-out theatre venues, entertained troops during World War II and finally turned to teaching magic.

In 1963, Verner moved into Hollywood's Magic Castle and held court there almost until the time of his death in 1992.

KATHERINE "KLONDIKE KATE" RYAN
1869–1932
The Good and Bad Klondike Gals

To the North-West Mounted Police, "proving up" was the required ticket into the Yukon gold fields during the rush of 1898. The NWMP required that every traveller into the territory have 400 pounds (181 kilograms) of flour, 150 pounds (68 kilograms) each of bacon, split peas, beans and tinned milk, as well as a sleeping bag, rifle, cooking pots and a Bible. Kate Ryan brought all that and more, along with the experience to use the proving-up supplies to feed others.

Katherine was a New Brunswick farm girl who knew about feeding hungry men and had worked her way west cooking in restaurants. A tall, strapping girl, she was called Klondike Kate from almost the first day of arriving in Whitehorse and even named her restaurant "Klondike Kate's." The miners got a fair deal at Klondike Kate's—her food and whisky were good and her pies were famously delicious. Kate was the apple of everyone's eye, including the poet and novelist Robert Service, who, as the rumour goes, got many of his story ideas from her. The North-West Mounted Police liked her so much that they made her their first woman special constable.

However, perhaps the strangest tale from the land of the midnight sun is the story of two Klondike Kates, for the original had a copycat in Seattle native Kitty Rockwell. Kitty, a popular dancehall girl, pawned herself off as Klondike Kate and, along with soon-to-be-famous theatre magnate Alexander

Pantages, became famous in the Yukon for bilking miners of their hard-earned gold. Years later, back in Seattle, Kitty Rockwell, still posing as Klondike Kate, sued theatre-owner Pantages for breach of marriage promise, a lawsuit that made the headlines. It led the original, straitlaced Klondike Kate Ryan to explain that a rose is not always a rose, especially in the land of the midnight sun.

LÉO-ERNEST OUIMET
1877–1972
The Father of Modern Cinema

Montréal electrical engineer Léo-Ernest Ouimet had a thing for lights, and in 1901, the 24-year-old rewired and installed innovative lighting in two of that city's theatres. The following year, he attended a Sunday night variety show at the city's 5000-seat, open-air pavilion in Sohmers Park, where he witnessed a demonstration of Edison's new projecting Kinetoscope. Intrigued, he contacted Edison, and in 1903, he received a distributorship for eastern Canada. Léo was happy with the arrangement, but not with Edison's projector, and within a year, he had fiddled the machine into projecting larger images and in a way that stopped the annoying flicker.

Léo called his improved projector the Ouimetoscope and took it on the road, doing outdoor shows in working-class neighbourhoods. These were large, well-attended affairs, and they gave Leo an idea—since his Ouimetoscope could project larger images inside as well as outdoors, why not show big pictures in some kind of theatre? Léo purchased an abandoned cabaret on Montréal's St. Catherine Street, gussied it up with red and gold paint and installed some innovative lighting along with 500 comfortable chairs. The theatre was such a hit that after a few years, he tore it down and built another with 1200 seats, calling it the "Ouimetoscope Theatre" after his improved projector. Léo put all the gold plaster and balconies found in ritzy legitimate theatres into his cathedral-sized movie house along with something new—air conditioning. He opened the Ouimetoscope Theatre on August 31, 1907, to a packed house and sold out every show for years. Future movie moguls came to Montréal from around the world to see Léo's fantastic theatre, and they would use his ideas in building their own grand movie palaces.

NATHAN L. NATHANSON
1896–1930
Canada's Movie-house Mogul

In 1920, Nathan L. Nathanson, a former Scarboro Beach Amusement Park concessionaire and founder of the Famous Players Canadian Corporation, the Canadian division of movie mogul Adolph Zukor's Paramount Pictures, opened the largest, most elaborate movie house in North America, Toronto's 3337-seat Pantages Theatre. Although Nathanson owned the Pantages, now called the Canon Theatre, Alexander Pantages handled the management and film bookings, and all the theatres in his circuit of 120 movie houses were called the Pantages. In both Canada and the U.S., Pantages monopolized theatres on the West Coast, while the Keith-Albee-Orpheum Corporation (KAO), held sway in the East. In 1922, to counter this monopoly, Nathanson acquired Léo-Ernest Ouimet's Specialty Film Import Company and featured many foreign films in his Famous Players theatres.

In 1929, to protest Adolph Zukor's plans to merge Famous Players with Paramount, Nathanson resigned, only to return in 1933 after the deal was deemed a violation of antitrust laws. In 1941, Nathan used his son Paul as a front to align himself with England's Rank Organization and form Odeon Pictures of Canada, an organization of independent theatre owners. Five years later, Nathanson sold Odeon Pictures to the Rank Organization and retired as one of Canada's wealthiest citizens. Not bad for a naturalized Canadian kid from Minneapolis who got his start selling cotton candy on the boardwalks of amusement parks.

VINA "FAY" WRAY
1907–2004
Our Queen of Scream

Born on a ranch in Cardston, Alberta, Fay Wray moved to Salt Lake City with her Mormon parents when she was five, and then to Hollywood, California, when she was 13.

She attended Hollywood High School, dabbled in local theatre and, in 1922, landed a spot in a newspaper-sponsored historical documentary. That led to minor roles in films such as *Gasoline Alley* in 1923 for Hal Roach Studios, and in 1925, she got a few major roles in pictures such as *Coast Patrol*, co-starring silent film heartthrob Ken MacDonald. Then she spent a year with Universal Studios doing low-budget westerns with cowboy co-star Buck Jones until Paramount grabbed her to star in a big-budget film called *The Wedding March*. The movie was a financial bust for Paramount, but they kept her onboard doing other films, mostly horror flicks, and she was one of the first actors to make the transition to talkies.

Film directors loved Fay—she was fun, always on time, knew her lines and never let alcohol affect her work. However, she was a bit naïve, and in 1933, when RKO Pictures producer Merian Cooper asked her to star in his new film, he explained that while her co-star had yet to be selected, her screen partner would defiantly be tall, dark and handsome. Although Cooper lied about the handsome part, King Kong was defiantly tall and dark. *King Kong* earned Fay the title "Queen of Scream," and at the film's debut, even she had to admit there was too much screaming. However, she would later happily point out that the picture saved RKO from bankruptcy. She also commented that she thought the monkey would haunt her future in film, and she was right, as her parts dwindled to occasional roles.

In 1942, she married and retired from acting, doing only the odd cameo or guest appearance. Fay would often return to her birthplace of Cardston and, today, on the town's main street, sits a memorial to its favourite daughter, a cool, bubbly water fountain.

ISRAEL HAROLD "IZZY" ASPER
1932–2003
Our Media Mogul

Born in Minnedosa, Manitoba, Izzy Asper graduated with a law degree from the University of Manitoba in 1964, setting up in Winnipeg as a tax specialist while authoring a nationally syndicated newspaper column on tax matters, an endeavour that led to an interest in both media and provincial politics. From 1970 to 1975, while serving as leader of the Manitoba Liberal Party, Asper and his business partner, Paul Morton, bought a foundering U.S. radio station and moved it to Winnipeg, where it became the phenomenally successful CKND. A few years later, Asper picked up another faltering media concern, the Global TV network, making it his flagship business and running it from a booth at The Velvet Glove steakhouse before moving to the top floor of Winnipeg's TD Centre, where he formed Canwest Global Communications.

In 1987, Asper used his media empire to undermine Brian Mulroney's political career and his control of the CBC by lambasting Mulroney's Meech Lake Accord attempt at fiddling with the constitution. Eventually, Asper had TV stations around the world, making him worth around $600 million. "Not enough," he thought, and in 2001, he bought Conrad Black's newspaper empire for $3.5 billion.

Asper called his customers "eyeballs," and though he had millions, he plugged away at acquiring more business while never leaving Winnipeg. He admitted to once being tempted to move to where the action was, but a phone call to Wal-Mart founder Sam Walton in Bentonville, Arkansas, set him straight when Sam explained that the rent for corporate offices in Bentonville was only $2 per square foot. At his death, Asper was worth well over a billion dollars.

RUTH LOWE
1914–81
A Songwriter for the Heart

Ruth Lowe started out as a "song plugger" at the Music Shop on Toronto's Yonge Street. She was 16 years old and the sole provider for her mother and little sister, her father having succumbed to pneumonia. Song pluggers played the newest songs for sheet music customers and took a cut of sales, not an easy job because the hours were long and the financial returns not great. To supplement her income, she worked nights playing at local nightclubs and radio stations and with local dance bands, jobs that led to a gig with Ina Ray Hutton's all-girl touring orchestra, the Melodears, the inspiration for the all-girl band in the movie *Some Like It Hot*.

That one-night gig became permanent, and at only 21 years of age, Ruth was a professional road musician. While travelling, she met, fell in love with and married Harold Cohen, a Chicago music publicist. Cohen died a year later during kidney surgery, and a very distraught Ruth returned to her mother's home on Barton Street in Toronto, where she put her grief to paper in a song called "I'll Never Smile Again." It was a tune for the times because World War II had many people thinking they would never smile again.

Ruth's friend Percy Faith had the first go at her song, arranging it in his smooth orchestral style, then the Dorsey Brothers got hold of it, and after creating an new arrangement for crooner Frank Sinatra, the melody was released on a record on May 23, 1940. It was Frank Sinatra's first recording, and "I'll Never Smile Again" became an instant hit and the first-ever number-one record on the new Billboard record chart. Listening to her song being sung and played everywhere by everybody freed Ruth from the doldrums, and she jumped into song writing with both feet. She composed more songs for Sinatra and other musicians, including Sinatra's signature song, "Put Your Dreams Away." Ruth was on top of the world, but on a visit home, she met Nat Sandler, a successful Toronto stockbroker, and fell in love. They married in 1945, and Ruth said goodbye to her days in the limelight.

RAYMOND WILLIAM STACEY BURR
1917–93
Perry Mason and Della Street, TV perfection

Born in New Westminster, British Columbia, Raymond Burr got his start playing bad guy Walt Radak in the movie *Desperate*. The role set the course for his future film parts until he hit the big time with the *Perry Mason* television series. In the early days, Hollywood required its actors to have a sterling public image, so to hide his sexual orientation, Raymond Burr invented his own biography, which included various marriages, a stint in U.S. military during World War II and a son who died of cancer. Not until biographer Michael Star published *In Plain Sight* in 2008 did the world come to know the real Raymond Burr. Not that it mattered because the man was a jewel—he gave to charities, supported orphaned kids, entertained troops in Korea and Vietnam. And who could not love a man who collected seashells?

WILLIAM ALAN "BILL" SHATNER
1931–
Beam Me Up, Scotty!

Born in Montréal, William Shatner has become to TV and films what peanut butter is to bread—ubiquitous. The guy never stops—he is everywhere, singing, directing, writing, selling and forever beaming up in *Star Trek* reruns and movies. A 1952 McGill University graduate, Bill is smart as a whip and loves games, tennis and horses, and if it's for charity and involves competition, Bill Shatner will be there—paintball, jogging, TV game shows, poker tournaments—you name it, and Bill's your man.

Shatner got his acting start a year before he graduated from college in a Canadian film called *The Butler's Night Out* in which he played an underworld hoodlum. He parlayed that experience into dozens of Broadway and film gigs before he hit the big time in 1959 in the Broadway production of *The World of Suzie Wong*. In 1962, he starred in producer-director Roger Corman's film *The Intruder*, a success that would be followed by many others. Shatner became friends with actor Leonard

Nimoy in 1964, and two years later, convinced Nimoy to don pointy ears and enter TV history as Mr. Spock in the sci-fi TV series *Star Trek*.

Shatner has been married four times. His first wife, Gloria Rand, divorced him in 1966 and took his three kids and every penny he made in the *Star Trek* series, forcing him to live out of a trailer for over a year. The most notable of his marriages, to Nerine Kidd, ended in tragedy when she drowned in the Shatners' swimming pool in 1999. Today, Shatner is happily married to Elizabeth Martin, with whom he shares a love of horses.

While doing the *Star Trek* series, Bill Shatner kept secret a horrible infirmity, one not revealed until his 2009 appearance on the *Tonight Show* with Conan O'Brien—he cannot split his fingers to perform the Vulcan salute. But what does that matter? He is still one of Canada's best and deserves to "live long and prosper."

EDWARD SAMUEL "TED" ROGERS JR.
1933–2008
He Liked His Name in Lights

In 1960, Ted Rogers Jr. jumped into specialty radio while still a student at Toronto's Osgoode Law School by buying radio station CHFI, a pioneer in FM radio. Five years later, he pioneered himself into cable TV, and in 1967, he formed Rogers Communication, a soon-to-be media giant.

In 2000, Rogers teamed up with Labatt Breweries to buy the Toronto Blue Jays baseball club, and by 2003, he owned not only the entire team, but also the wonderful stadium they played in, which he promptly renamed the Rogers Centre. Rogers liked seeing his name on big-ticket items, and in 2007, when he and wife Loretta donated $15 million to Ryerson University, it was on the condition that the faculty of business was renamed the Ted Rogers School of Management.

Ted Rogers passed away at only 76 years young, and if he had lived another 10 years, there is little doubt that Toronto would have been named Rogers City. We miss you Ted—things are not the same with you gone.

CHARLES "STOMPIN' TOM" CONNORS
1936–
Wild in the Country

Weird, wonderful and rabidly Canadian, Stompin' Tom hails from St. John, New Brunswick. Seized from his teenage mother, he was adopted by a family in Skinner's Pond, PEI, from where he and his guitar hit the road in 1951. Tom hitchhiked cross-country, taking odd jobs and writing songs about

the things he saw and the people he met. The early 1960s found him stompin' steady at the Maple Leaf Hotel in Timmins, Ontario, with a spot on a local radio station, a fortuitous gig that led to him make eight records. In 1969, he signed with Dominion Records and released six albums, and two years later, he formed his own record company, Boot Records, and released 10 more albums, many of which garnered him Juno Awards.

In 1979, Tom released his last album, and in a fit of rage over the Americanization of the Canadian music industry, he returned all six of his Junos and retired from the business. Gone but not out, Stompin' Tom popped up from nowhere in 1986 to announce that he had signed with EMI Records for the release of his entire song collection. He was awarded the Order of Canada in 1986, and St. Thomas University in New Brunswick gave him credit for his education in the school of life by granting him an honorary Doctor of Laws degree in 1993.

GUY LALIBERTÉ
1959–
Our King of Fun

Born in Québec City, Guy Laliberté was taken by his parents to a Ringling Brothers and Barnum & Bailey Circus in 1968, and Guy knew what he wanted to be when he grew up. After the school day ended, he busked on the streets of Québec City, playing his accordion and harmonica and mingling with other street performers, who taught him fire breathing, stilt walking and juggling. He had talent and was soon touring with a small troupe of performers, a kind of circus without lions and tigers made popular in the 19th century by legendary Québec show-man Gustave Lambert. Laliberté called his ensemble Cirque du Soleil, a name conceived while he was on vacation in sunny Hawaii. Aided by mentor Gilles Ste-Croix and a grant from the Québec government, Cirque du Soleil soon hit the big time and today employs over 4000 people, putting on shows around the world and generating revenues of almost $1 billion.

Banking millions had little effect on Laliberté, and he has remained a fun-loving, hands-on operator, but his success has allowed him to indulge in his favourite pastime, high-stakes poker, a game he excels at. In 2008, tired of vacationing in Hawaii, Laliberté contracted with the Russians for a look at the world from a different perspective, and in 2009, he became Canada's first space tourist, circling the globe for 12 days in a Soyuz space capsule.

Less flamboyant about his philanthropic activities, Laliberté contributes both his time and his millions to the One Drop Foundation, an initiative to improve the lives of people living in developing countries by providing clean drinking water.

K.D. LANG
1961–
Hot Sauce in Pablum

Born Kathryn Dawn Lang in Edmonton, Alberta, k.d., who insists her name be spelled with lowercase letters, always loved singing for family and friends. She found a niche while at college in Red Deer, Alberta, when she discovered the songs of country singer Patsy Kline. In 1983, she formed a Patsy Kline tribute band called The Reclines and cut her first album, *Friday Dance Promenade*. The music worked, but her seven-hour-long, on-tour reenactment of a heart transplant was a dismal head scratcher, as was her 1985 acceptance of a Juno Award while wearing a wedding dress that made her look like a splash of hot sauce in a bowl of Pablum.

In need of guidance, k.d. signed with a Nashville record producer in 1986, a fortuitous arrangement that gave the world her *Angel With a Lariat* album and a duet rerecording of "Crying" with Roy Orbison. K.d. was now into the big time, and in 1990, the vegan artist used her popularity to launch an attack on meat eating that so enraged Alberta beef producers they financed a media smear campaign that prompted her to admit that she was gay and sent her into hiding for a while. But in 1992, she was back to release the swing album *Ingénue*, with its monster hits "Constant Craving" and "Chatelaine" for which the recording industry heaped on the awards. The supermarket tabloids had a field day, associating k.d. with dozens of female celebrities, and she cultivated the controversy by dressing in a manly style.

Swing, country, pop, crooner—our k.d. does it all, both solo and partnered with top talent such as her pal Tony Bennett. Today, the weird and wonderful k.d. resides in Los Angeles with two dogs and a girlfriend in a house once owned by actor

Rock Hudson. She actively campaigns for gay and animal rights and still does occasional concert tours.

JAMES EUGENE "JIM" CARREY
1962–
Our Bigger-than-life Funnyman

Toronto-born Jim Carrey's motto has always been "Turn your wheels into the skid, kid," and with that attitude, he has triumphed to become a king of schizo-comedy through his portrayal of characters with major social adjustment problems, the most famous being pet detective Ace Ventura and Stanley Ipkiss, the Mask character. No flash-in-the-pan actor, Carrey has worked himself from stand-up comedy to the big screen by sheer determination and the ability to release his manic alter ego at a moment's notice. However, like Stanley Ipkiss in the movie *Mask*, Jim Carrey has a problem putting aside his inner funny man, a fact attested to by two failed marriages and a history of dead-end romances.

MICHAEL JOHN "MIKE" MYERS
1963–
Our "Mini Me"

Possessed with the spirit of an ancestral Scottish gnome, Toronto-born Mike Myers turned the frozen puck and its aficionados into comedic legend, first on *Saturday Night Live* and then as Wayne Campbell in the two *Wayne's World* films. Unlike his fellow comedian and countryman Jim Carrey, Myers has no problem putting his alter egos aside. He emulates Groucho Marx by introducing his invented characters to stand-up audiences, and then dropping them if they fail to please the masses.

During the mid-1970s, before there was Mike Myers the actor, there was Myers the consummate joker, who, rumour has it, once tried to avoid a charge of rowdy-ism by slipping the cop a Monopoly "Get Out of Jail Free" card. And who but Myers could be the voice of Shrek and get away with ordering the seven dwarfs to get Snow White off his kitchen table, "Oh, no, no, no, no! Dead broad *off* the table."

ALANIS NADINE MORRISETTE
1974–
Our Mrs. Souleye

Born in Ottawa, Alanis demonstrated musical talent at an early age, becoming proficient on both piano and guitar by her teens. She also became proficient with drugs and alcohol, the subjects of her monster hit album *Jagged Little Pill*, which was released after she moved to Los Angeles in 1995 and signed with Madonna's Maverick Records.

A year later, overwhelmed by success, she ran away to India to do good, hang around soaking up karma and hum mantras in local ashrams. In 1998, she returned to Canada with a new song, "Uninvited," which probably sums up her India venture. After playing God in the 1999 movie *Dogma*, a reporter asked her if she had ever read the Bible, and she replied, "Sure, and I found it patriarchal and sexist."

In 2010, Alanis married rapper Mario "Souleye" Treadway, and the couple named their first child Ever, as in, if this relationship ever lasts more than a year, it will be a miracle.

BORN IN CANADA MAJOR FILM OSCAR WINNERS
Our Stars of the Silver Screen

Mary Pickford (Toronto, ON) — Best Actress, *Coquette* (1929)

Norma Shearer (Montréal, QC) — Best Actress, *The Divorcee* (1930)

Douglas Shearer (Montréal, QC) — Best Sound Recording, *The Big House* (1930)

Marie Dressler (Cobourg, ON) — Best Actress, *Min and Bill* (1931)

Richard Day (Victoria, BC) — Best Art Direction, *The Dark Angel* (1935), *Dodsworth* (1936), *How Green Was My Valley* (1941), *My Gal Sal* (1942), *This Above All* (1943), *A Streetcar Named Desire* (1951), *On the Waterfront* (1954)

Mack Sennett (Danville, QC)	Best Live Action Short Film, *Wrestling Swordfish* (1931), Academy Honorary Award (1938)
Deanna Durbin (Winnipeg, MB)	Academy Juvenile Award (1939)
Harold Russell (North Sydney, NS)	Best Supporting Actor, *The Best Years of Our Lives* (1946)
Walter Huston (York County, ON)	Best Supporting Actor, *The Treasure of the Sierra Madre* (1948)
James Cameron (Kapuskasing, ON)	Best Picture and Best Director, *Titanic* (1997)
Paul Haggis (London, ON)	Best Picture, Best Original Screenplay, *Crash* (2004)

Our Heroes
and Heroines

Historians are prone to calling Canada's exceptional
people "heroes" or "heroines" if they did anything at all
extraordinary, but that defies the true definition of the
word "hero," which means "to commit an act of distinguished courage and selflessness in the face of adversity."
How many Canadians fit that description? Most of
us will think of Laura Secord and her long walk to
warn the British of an impending U.S. attack during
the War of 1812, an undertaking amplified and made
heroic by a chocolate company. Laura's walk, though
long and arduous, was short on adversity because she
was at no time in any danger. On the other hand, we
have 13-year-old Cornelia de Grassi, who chose to go
and get vital information, was constantly in danger and
returned with that information in a hail of gunfire—
a real heroine who has largely gone unrecognized for
her deed.

SARAH "SALLY" AINSE
1728–1823
Our Stealthy Spy

They called her Oneida Sally, and when she moved to south-western Ontario in 1766, she brought along both her trading acumen and her political shrewdness. Sally traded with tribes from Lake Erie south to the Ohio area of the U.S. that today comprises the states of Ohio, Michigan, Illinois, Indiana and Wisconsin, and she won the respect of everyone she dealt with. In the years following the end of the American Revolutionary War in 1783, the government of George Washington began moving to wrest control of the Ohio Country from the Native Americans, and in 1794, General "Mad" Anthony Wayne was let loose on the Native Americans with instructions to destroy them and push north. General Wayne, with a force of 3000 Kentucky sharpshooters, defeated the Confederation of Tribes at the Battle of Fallen Trees, resulting in a massive British reinforcement of Canada West in preparation for a push north by Wayne's forces.

The British needed information, and through Chief Joseph Brant, they got it via Oneida Sally, who made dangerous trips south to spy on Wayne's forces. It was on her recommendation, since she reported that tribes once opposed to Wayne were now aligning with him and could not be counted on to support the British, that the Treaty of Greenville was signed in 1795. The treaty ceded control of the Ohio Country to the U.S., stopping what would have inevitably been a northward invasion into Canada by General "Mad Anthony" Wayne and his troops.

CORNELIA DE GRASSI
1814–85
She Saved "Bonehead's" Bacon

Filippo "Phillip" de Grassi, an Italian officer serving in the Grand Army of France, was captured by British forces during an early battle of the Peninsula War, Napoleon's ill-fated 1804–14 attempt to subjugate Portugal. Taken to England and paroled, de Grassi obtained a captaincy in the York Light Infantry Volunteers in 1812 and served out his contract in the British West Indies. Returning to England in 1815, he taught languages, got married and had two daughters, Cornelia and Charlotte. In 1831, taking advantage of land grants available to British officers, he took his family to York (present-day Toronto) and settled on a section of land on the east side of the Don River not far from the Todmorden Mills, where he planted apple orchards.

Officers with land grants, especially those with Freemasonry affiliations like de Grassi, were expected to contribute time to militia duty, and de Grassi devoted himself so fully to the task that the politically discontented William Lyon Mackenzie made him privy to intrigues against the Upper Canada government of Sir Francis Bond Head. In 1937, word arrived at York that well-armed Mackenzie supporters were gathering from around the province at Montgomery's Tavern north of the city and were preparing to march on York. The news put Governor Bond Head into a panic because all the British military forces had been sent to Lower Canada to put down revolts, and he was left with only a small militia unit, Phillip de Grassi's men.

Governor Bond Head prepared to abandon the city but was convinced to wait while de Grassi reconnoitred the enemy's strength, a difficult task because Yonge Street, the only road to Montgomery's Tavern, was barricaded at several places. De Grassi needed to get spies into the very centre of Mackenzie's mob, and it seemed so impossible a task that Bond Head ordered a ship made ready to depart at a moment's notice. However, fate interceded when de Grassi's daughters got word from a friend working at the Todmorden paper mill that Mackenzie had ordered paper to be delivered to Montgomery's Tavern.

"We can take it," said Cornelia and Charlotte. "We know the area, and no one will suspect two girls delivering paper."

Having no alternative, de Grassi agreed, but only allowed his youngest daughter and better rider, Cornelia, to make the attempt. The girl left the paper mill at first light and rode up Yonge Street, passing through rebel roadblocks with little difficulty. After delivering the paper, she got a good look at the insurrectionists and determined that they were completely unprepared for battle. They were too lightly armed, half drunk and without rations. This was information she had to get to her father, but there was a problem. Mackenzie had issued orders that once in, nobody should be allowed to leave.

In spite of the danger, Cornelia took to her horse and, keeping low in the saddle, rode hell for leather through a hail of bullets into Toronto history. Her report that their opponents were poorly armed, drunk and hungry stopped Bond Head's exodus from Toronto and sent de Grassi's militia north to hold the rebel advance until help arrived from Hamilton.

ABIGAIL BECKER
1830–1905
Our Lady of the Lake

They called her the "Angel of Long Point," and for good reason, because she single-handedly and at great personal risk saved dozens of seaman from watery graves in the treacherous waters of Lake Erie at Long Point.

Originally from New York State, Abigail moved to Norfolk County, Ontario, with her family, and in 1848, at only 17 years of age, she married widower and Long Point trapper Jeremiah Becker, acquiring a ready-made family of five boys and a daughter. Becker built a cabin from driftwood for his family near the tip of Long Point, and though it was isolated, Abigail loved it. During her first winter, with snow blowing, the wind howling and her husband off on a supply run, Abigail's solitude was broken by the sudden appearance at her door of four half-frozen seamen who explained that two of their mates had collapsed along the way. Out she went into the storm, and with the help of two of her boys, she succeeded in finding the two men and dragging them back to the cabin, saving their lives.

In November 1854, in the midst of a terrific storm, Abigail ventured out to retrieve a bucket of water from the lake and spotted a ship's boat overturned on the shore. Thinking the worst, she waited for dawn and ran for miles along the beach, dodging huge breakers until she happened upon the schooner *Conductor* hard aground on a sandbar half a mile from shore, her decks awash and her crew of eight tied into the high rigging. After waving at the half-frozen men, she turned and headed home, returning as quickly as she could with her children and supplies to aid in the sailors' rescue. They built a huge fire, and while not a swimmer, Abigail, tied to the end of a rope, braved the enormous surf, getting close enough to yell encouragement to the men. They came reluctantly, their captain first, and Abigail was there to help them ashore one by one.

For her heroism, Lake Erie's ships captains honoured Abigail with a grand banquet in Buffalo, New York, and presented her with a purse of $500, money contributed by grateful seamen. Queen Victoria sent her a nice letter along with $50, and the Benevolent Life Saving Association of New York presented Abigail with a solid gold medal engraved with a picture of her Long Point cabin.

Abigail Becker, the Angel of Long Point, was the sort of person everyone hopes will be on the beach in times of trouble.

NELLIE LETITIA McCLUNG
1873–1951
She Tossed a Mean Tomato

Born Nellie Letitia Mooney in Chatsworth, a small village in southwestern Ontario, Nellie moved with her family in 1880 to homestead a tract of land on the Souris River near Brandon, Manitoba. In 1882, she attended school for the first time, and by the age of 15, she had her teacher's certificate. A year later, Nellie met women's activist Annie McClung, who pointed her way to the future. Nellie also met Annie's son, whom she married a few years later.

Under Annie's tutelage, Nellie wrote a book called *Sowing Seeds in Danny*, a bestseller that stressed the sad situation of both Canadian and immigrant women—no vote and no property rights, with many immigrant women workers treated as slaves. In fact, women in Manitoba and across Canada were not even recognized as being persons.

Nellie set out to rectify these issues by hitting the road and speaking to women's groups, for which she soon garnered the name "suffragette" and the animosity of Manitoba's male population, who would turn out and pelt the ladies with overripe tomatoes. However, with Nellie yelling encouragement, the women would pick up the tossed tomatoes and throw them back at the men most vigorously.

Nellie wrote more books and toured the country, speaking out against inequality and alcoholism, and by 1916, after participating in a hugely successful mock parliament in which women denied men the right to vote, she won women the right to vote, first in Manitoba, and then in Alberta. The next year, she helped cajole Ottawa politicians into allowing the mothers and wives of servicemen to vote, and by the end of World War I, she was in Alberta and had won a seat in the provincial legislature. In 1929, as member of the West's "Famous Five," along with Emily Murphy, Irene Parlby, Louise

McKinney and Henrietta Muir Edwards, she won the right of Canadian women to be called "persons" in a lawsuit decided by Britain's Privy Council.

Nellie McClung defied adversity along with a blizzard of tomatoes to gain equal rights for women and become a legendary Canadian heroine.

DID YOU KNOW?

By 1906, the Plains bison that once numbered around 60 million animals had been hunted nearly to extinction, with the last remaining herd of 800 beasts assembled and protected by Métis ranchers Charles Allard and Michel Pablo at Montana's Flatland Reservation. When word reached Ottawa that the Allard-Pablo herd was for sale, they jumped at the opportunity and sent Alexandre Ayotte, a former Montana immigration agent, to broker the deal. Ayotte bought 716 animals at $245 each and spent years transporting the animals to Canada for dispersal to various park, reestablishing herds that have grown from almost none to over 10,000 animals.

Our
Inscrutables

The dictionary defines "inscrutable" as being mysterious or not easily understood, or perhaps doing something that would prompt others to ask, "Why would anyone do such a crazy thing?" Many weird and wonderfully inscrutable Canadians were motivated by king and country, while others were looking for fame or riches. Some simply pursued the unusual for its own sake and for the fun it provided.

SIR MATTHEW BAILLIE BEGBIE
1819–94

All a Judge Needs Is a Good Horse and a Tall Tree

They called him a "hanging judge," and at 6 feet, 5 inches (196 centimetres) tall, the pistol-packing, opera-singing BC judge scared the hell out of criminals whenever he rode into a mining town. An Englishman by birth, Begbie graduated from Cambridge University with an arts degree, studied law at Lincoln's Inn and opened a London law office. A bit bored with practising law in England, he jumped at the chance when the Crown offered him a legal position in their newly formed Colony of British Columbia. Begbie arrived at Fort Victoria on November 16, 1858, three years before the Fraser Canyon Gold Rush began.

The gold rush kept him busy, and since crime was widespread in the region, Begbie took the law to settlements and mining towns on foot and horseback. A talented artist, he used the travel time between courts to map the land, draw imaginary bridges and illustrate BC flora. Begbie was also good with languages, especially those of the First Nations. Wearing his ubiquitous black robe and powdered wig, he would hear testimony from Aboriginal people in their own tongues while drawing their pictures from his position on the bench. He hung all murderers, claim jumpers and mail robbers, and sentenced those who committed lesser crimes to work on community projects. Some historians claim that before entering a settlement for the first time, he would scout the periphery for a suitable hanging tree. Others have stated that he was not above accepting financial inducements for suitable verdicts and cite the Cottonwood Scandal, in which Begbie somehow acquired 20 acres (8 hectares) of prime development land near Quesnel, British Columbia.

During an 1875 visit to England, the judge garnered a knighthood and returned to BC as Sir Matthew Begbie, Supreme Court Justice, a job he held until his death in 1894. The province put him into the ground in a fashion befitting the man they considered to be BC's first citizen, with almost the entire city of Victoria turning out for the ceremony.

JOHN ANGUS "CARIBOO" CAMERON
1820–88
A Solid Gold Husband

Born in Charlottenburgh, Canada West, a village on the St. Lawrence River, John and his two brothers succumbed to gold fever in 1852 and set off for California to make their fortunes. Six years later, the three returned home with

$20,000 in gold, which the brothers used to buy farms. John married his childhood love, Sophia Groves, and a year later, when news arrived of a gold strike in British Columbia, Sophia and John, along with their four-month-old baby girl, packed up and headed west to get their share.

John's second trip to look for gold would, sadly, not prove as fortuitous as his first venture. The baby died the following year in Victoria, BC, at about the same time as John and his partner, Robert Stevenson, were seeing some colour in their claim on William's Creek. John and Sophia buried their little girl and set off for the claim, but upon reaching it, Sophia came down with typhoid. On her deathbed, Sophia elicited a promise from John not to bury her in the wilds, but to take her body home to the family vault. When she passed away, John put her into a coffin and stored the body in an outbuilding while he turned his attention to the claim. In January 1863, John loaded the coffin and a 50-pound (23-kilogram) bag of gold onto a toboggan and, along with his partner and 20 miners hired to drag it, set off on the 600-mile (966-kilometre) journey back to Victoria.

The weather turned miserably cold, and upon reaching Quesnel, the draggers deserted, but John and Robert were able to purchase a horse and continue their journey. The trip to Victoria took over two months, and John and his partner were anxious to get back to their claim before jumpers took it over. John transferred Sophia's body into a specially made tin coffin, had an undertaker dump in 25 gallons (95 litres) of embalming fluid and buried her in the cemetery next to their infant daughter.

Back at the claim, it was bonanza time, and within six months, John had taken out $250,000 in gold. He returned to Victoria to dig up Sophia, put her into a brand-new mahogany coffin and take her home to Charlottenburgh. His promise kept, John built a large mansion, remarried and lived happily ever after—but not quite, because folks was a-talkin'. The scuttlebutt was that he had traded his wife to a Native chief for gold, and the coffin he buried was empty. It was all nonsense, but newspapers picked up the story and blew it out of proportion. The public embarrassment became too much for John, and he announced a coffin opening to be attended by relatives and anyone else who was interested. People came in droves, and when the coffin lid was opened, there was Sophia, dressed in her Sunday best and looking fresh as a daisy. Seeing her looking almost alive took a toll on poor John, and after his investments soured in 1886, he returned to the BC goldfields, hoping to refill his purse. But he arrived there a sick and broken man, and died in Victoria two years later.

GEORGE DENISON
1839–1925
What Goes Around, Comes Around

In 1865, Canadian authorities boarded the steamship *Georgian* at Collingwood, Ontario, and found George Denison, scion of a prominent Toronto family, a lawyer and a colonel of militia busily preparing the ship to receive a cannon that had been stolen from the town of Guelph. Authorities seized the ship, but after Denison denied that it was being prepared to attack northern U.S. Civil War POW camps, he sued for its return. The suit was joined by the Americans, who demanded the ship as a prize of war since it had been purchased using Confederate funds.

Denison lost the suit and was so peeved that he formed a group called the "Twelve Apostles" and also founded the Canada First political party to harass John A. Macdonald over his plans for Confederation. Denison's efforts were instrumental in prompting Macdonald to hang the Métis insurrectionist Louis Riel. To get rid of Denison, the government sent him to England as Immigration Commissioner, where he happily hobnobbed with the gentry and wrote a book that prophesied the end of cavalry in the military. In 1877, his friend and Ontario premier, Oliver Mowat, offered Denison the post of police magistrate for the city of Toronto, a post that he held for the next four decades.

PROFESSOR CHARLES HENRY DANIELLE
1830–1902
Our Dance Master

A real castle it was not, but in middle-of-nowhere Newfoundland, it made the grade in three respects: its unusually tall, octagonal shape, its multitude of gaily decorated rooms and its host, the corpulent and effervescent Professor Charles Henry Danielle. Originally from Chicago, where he had operated a successful dance academy, Danielle moved to St. John's, Newfoundland, in about 1875. There he engaged in profitable business ventures that included leasing a skating rink, from which he conducted fancy dress balls and ice carnivals, renting costumes to those attending the events.

In 1878, fire consumed his rink and costumes, but the flamboyant Professor was adequately insured and used the payoff to construct the Royal Lake Pavilion, a sumptuous roadhouse hotel on Quidi Vidi Lake just east of St. John's. Danielle inexplicably dismantled his palace in 1895 and shipped it by rail to middle-of-nowhere Irvine Station, where he reconstructed the edifice into a towering, octagon-shaped hotel that he called the Octagon Castle. The grand but oddly shaped hotel had an excess of 10,000 square feet (929 square metres) of interior space, with every room panelled and wallpapered in a different style. By 1900, almost 10,000 people had visited the hotel, either as guests or tourists.

His visitors all knew that Danielle was not long for this world because one room was devoted to the display of his glass coffin. The Professor suffered from a leaky heart valve, and though doctors had advised him to rest to prolong his days, he persevered in doing what he loved, entertaining the public, with his glass coffin becoming a major attraction. In 1901, in a booklet he distributed to guests, Danielle prophesized that his next season would be his last, and true to form, he succumbed to an attack of hiccups and passed into that great dancehall in the sky. The Professor's glass coffin allowed attendees at his funeral one last look at the man who taught Newfoundlanders that there was more to dancing than the jig.

KOOTENAI BROWN
1839–1916
He Found Paradise

Born John George Brown in Ireland and raised by his grandparents, Brown received a commission in the British Army in 1857, serving for a time in India. In 1861, he sold his commission and headed off to the goldfields of British Columbia to find his fortune. He never found gold, but in 1862, he found something almost as good—oil.

Curious about the black, tar-like substance used in various ways by an indigenous tribe in the Crowsnest Pass area of Alberta, Brown asked to be shown the place where it seeped from the ground. He called the spot Oil Creek, and after constructing a cabin there, he went to work dipping gunnysacks into the seep and squeezing the oil into one-gallon (4.5-litre) containers. Brown, a gold miner, fur trapper, guide and gunslinger, is probably least known for the fact that he was the first in Alberta to collect, bottle and commercially market oil. He sold it as a wagon wheel lubricant, and in 1874, he filed an affidavit to assert his rights of discovery on Oil Creek.

In 1879, Brown moved to Alberta's marvellous Waterton Lakes area and began lobbying Ottawa to protect its grandeur by having it declared a national park. In an odd twist, Waterton Lakes National Park is named for Charles Waterton, a British ornithologist who never laid eyes on the place that Kootenai Brown discovered in 1859 while guiding for the Palliser expedition of English naturalists.

DID YOU KNOW?

In 1866, a band of Cree bestowed a great honour on missionary and author John McDougall by taking him to the banks of the Iron River, near Killam, Alberta, to see the Cree and Blackfoot's most sacred possession, the Manitou Stone. Set on a pedestal and surrounded by offerings, the conical stone reflected sunlight off its metallic surface in a geometric pattern, with sections resembling a human face.

McDougall knew the stone to be a meteorite, and having read stories of the Muslim-venerated Black Stone relic in the holy city of Mecca and fearing an impediment to the spread of Christianity among the Cree and Blackfoot, he repaid their trust by stealing the Manitou Stone. His theft, according to Cree medicine men, doomed the Plains First Nations to war, disease and famine. Shortly after McDougall's crime, war erupted between the Cree and the Blackfoot, smallpox ravaged the Plains tribes and the bison herds began to dwindle.

During the 1880s, the Manitou Stone was sent to Victoria University in Cobourg, Ontario, for study, and though it remains their property, it is now back in Alberta on display at the Royal Alberta Museum in Edmonton and is deemed too scientifically important to be returned to the Cree.

EMILY PAULINE JOHNSON
1861–1913
The "Indian Princess" Who Wasn't

Born on the Six Nations Reserve near Brantford, Ontario, to a Mohawk father and an English mother, Pauline Johnson worked herself up from amateur thespian and part-time journalist to become one of the consummate female stage performers of the 19th century. She made her first appearance onstage as a prim and proper Englishwoman dressed in a ball-gown, and then as a Native "princess" dressed in Mohawk regalia while reciting galvanizing poetry to her audience. During the early 1890s, Pauline toured the U.S. and sold out every venue, and then she was off to England, where she hob-nobbed with royalty and recited poetry to packed audiences.

Pauline Johnson's poems struck at the public consciousness over the treatment of North America's indigenous peoples and lamented the folly of sacrificing what could have been a great relationship to greed and avarice. Pauline was the "Indian princess who wasn't," and in 1907, she moved to Vancouver, where she spent her last days living with the Squamish tribe and writing books and articles for magazines. In her will, Pauline asked that her ashes be cast into Stanley Park, a request that the city was more than happy to fulfill.

Dream of tender gladness,
Of filmy sun and opal-tinted skies
And warm midsummer air that lightly lies
In mystic rings.

–Pauline Johnson, poet

ARCHIBALD STANSFELD "ARCHIE" BELANEY, GREY OWL
1888–1938
The "Indian" Who Wasn't

In 1908, 20-year-old English immigrant Archibald Belaney married a full-blood Ojibwa woman named Angele Egwuna and promised her a white girl's future. Angele was having none of that and countered with a promise to make Archie into an

Ojibwa. That was fine by Archie, so Angele began the process that would turn him into what the world would come to believe was a full-blood Ojibwa.

An accomplished canoeist and trapper, Archie was soon living with Angele's family and acting very much like an Ojibwa. To complete his transformation, the Englishman tied his hair into a ponytail and took an Ojibwa name, Wa-sha-quon-asin, which means "White Beaked Owl." The name suited Archie's long-nosed countenance, but he later told people that it meant "He Who Walks by Night." He then settled on the moniker Grey Owl, the name the world would know him by.

Archie and Angele had a daughter named Agnes, and after three years of family life, Archie inexplicably packed up and moved to Biscotasing, Ontario. Although local Ojibwa knew he was not one of theirs, the whites thought he was

Aboriginal, and it was a charade that Archie perpetuated by dying his hair, staining his skin and speaking Ojibwa. Archie was never big on truth, except when it came to environmental issues, and he would later take those into the world like a sacred trust.

In 1914, Archie moved in with Marie Gérard, a Métis woman. The union produced a son, John, and a year later, Archie enlisted in the army. As a First Nations man who was good with a rifle, he was made a sniper and sent to the front, but not long afterward, he was a patient in an English hospital, having suffered what was probably a self-inflicted foot wound. There he met Ivy Holmes, a childhood friend, and after a few months, they married, with Archie keeping mum about his Canadian relationships. Archie returned to Canada alone, leaving Ivy to believe that she would soon follow, even though she never did. Archie spent a few years in Biscotasing honing his Native persona and drinking whisky with local trappers.

In 1925, he moved to Temagami and took up with Angele again, but the following year, he left his pregnant wife again and headed for Québec. There he took up with a lovely, young Iroquois girl named Gertrude Bernard, who Archie renamed Anahareo. The girl was a turning point in Archie's life because she loved animals and her mother, and Anahareo soon had Archie loving them as well and writing to his own mother in England, whom he had not contacted in 35 years. Mum liked the letters so much she sent them to *Country Life* magazine, and the editors requested more, along with articles.

Back in Canada, Anahareo had adopted two beaver kits that she named McGinty and McGinnis, and they became the focal point of Archie's new Native writer persona. He wrote from the mind of a "noble savage" in the wilds of Canada, and his British readers lapped it up. His writing soon attracted the attention of the Canadian Parks Service; they were making films to attract tourists to their parks and the tall, handsome, eloquent Archie Belaney fit the bill as spokesman so perfectly that, in 1930, they gave him a cabin in Saskatchewan's Riding Mountain National Park. Archie wrote a book for *Country Life*, penned a bestseller, and his film was shown around the world. He went on speaking tours of England, the U.S. and Canada, and for almost three hours, he would hold audiences spellbound with tales of the Canadian wilderness while extolling the virtues of conservation. Archie did a lot for the environment—he got the Parks Service to hire more First Nations people as rangers, curtailed tree cutting and trapping in certain areas and cajoled politicians into creating new parks.

Archie became our environmental conscience, and by 1932, he was Canada's greatest celebrity. He wrote, made films and toured as a full-blood Mohawk. Touring was a bit lonely for Archie, so he got married again, this time to a French Canadian girl from Ottawa named Yvonne Perrier, for which he created another persona, that of Archie McNeil, to avoid being found a bigamist.

By 1937, Archie's whisky drinking was causing him problems with the Parks Department, and he left for a speaking tour of England, taking Yvonne along as Princess Silver Moon. The Parks Department was no longer interested in Archie as a film star, but they kept quiet about his dual personality to protect his image, as did the *North Bay Nugget* newspaper after Angele, the only one of Archie's wives who knew his secret, spilled the beans to reporters.

Archie Belaney as Grey Owl was one of the greatest impersonations in history, with the curtain finally going down in that little cabin in Saskatchewan, where Archie Belaney drank himself to death in 1938.

CHARLES VANCE MILLAR
1853–1926
The Joke Was on Them

Toronto resident Charles Millar chose law as a profession, and though that proved successful, he made most of his considerable fortune from investments in British Colombia real estate ventures. Unmarried, affable and with a lifelong penchant for pranks, Millar shocked Toronto society by leaving a will that contained more than a few practical jokes. He left shares in the Ontario Jockey Club to two socially prominent Torontonians who had publicly condemned the sport and a similar number of shares to a man who had been denied Jockey Club membership for having a less-than-staunch reputation. Millar willed his shares in the O'Keefe Brewing Company, a Catholic-owned business, to Protestant ministers and Orange Order members, and a house in Jamaica was left to three lawyers who hated each other.

However, his biggest joke lay in clause 9 of his will, wherein he left the bulk of his estate to the woman who could bear the most children in a 10-year period. The initial amount was $100,000; however, by the time the contest had run its course in 1936, the value of the shares in the estate had risen to an astounding $750,000. Legal battles ensued, but in the end, four women received $125,000 each for bearing nine children, with the remainder going to lawyers' fees and to settle various lawsuits from spurious claimants.

ROBERT BALDWIN "ROBBIE" ROSS
1869–1918
Robbie and Oscar Go to the Fair

As the son of Deputy Premier of Canada Robert Baldwin, Robbie Ross would have been destined for greatness if not for his sexual orientation. Ross attended Cambridge University in England, where he was never shy about his homosexuality, a fact that caused him endless problems. He dropped out of school and returned to Canada, planning to work for his father, but all he received was a cold shoulder, a return ticket to England and an allowance.

Back in London, Ross found work as a journalist and critic, and through those endeavours, he met famed novelist and prime wit Oscar Wilde. The two became lifelong friends, and after Wilde's demise, Ross bought up all of his friend's manuscripts for posterity and paid for the famous writer's mausoleum, making sure there was a small niche in which to tuck his own ashes. Oscar Wilde and his weird and wonderful Canadian soulmate, Robbie Ross, are together now in the great forever.

AIMEE SEMPLE McPHERSON
1890–1944
She Stuck to Her Story

Aimee Elizabeth Kennedy was born in Salford, near London, Ontario, into a farming family whose matriarch was a tireless worker for the Salvation Army. In high school, Aimee learned Darwinian evolution, a theory she was vehemently opposed to because of her religious beliefs, and she decided to heed the word of God and spread it everywhere. In 1907, while attending a Pentecostal revival meeting, she met Robert James Semple, an Irish evangelist, and married him the following year. The pair embarked immediately on an evangelical tour of Europe and China.

In China, Aimee lost her husband to malaria and returned to North America to live with her mother, who had moved to

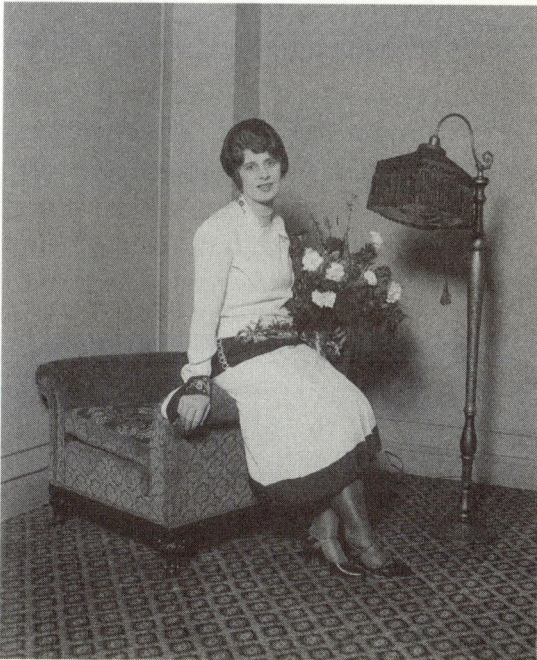

New York City. There she began to conduct revival meetings and toured the U.S. and Canada to standing-room-only crowds. Aimee Semple was a firebrand preacher who put on a great show, and in San Diego, California, they had to call out the National Guard to control a crowd of over 30,000. With so much money pouring in from contributions, she soon needed an accountant, and Harold Stewart McPherson did such a good job that she married him.

In 1916, Aimee and Harold hit the road in the "Gospel Car," a 1912 Packard touring car covered with religious signage, and she would stand up in the backseat and shout sermons through a megaphone. Building on her success, Aimee started a magazine, *The Bridal Call*, in which she wrote articles about the role of women in religion. It was all getting to be a bit much for husband Harold, and in 1918, he filed for divorce. Aimee kept his name and once again hit the road, landing in Baltimore, where she packed the Lyric Opera House for a month straight and garnered a heap of media attention.

Raking in the dough, Aimee set her sights on a brick-and-mortar church, and on January 1, 1923, the Angelus Temple, located in the heart of Los Angeles, became reality, with a capacity audience of 5300 faithful and Aimee right up front, perched on a velvet-covered throne. She called her organization the International Church of the Foursquare Gospel, and attendees at the temple were treated to a show on a professionally designed set with a hip choir. At the entrance to Aimee's grand temple stood a big sign that read "No coins, please," and the money rolled in almost faster than it could be counted. She soon had her own radio station but lost the licence in 1925.

By 1926, Aimee Semple McPherson was the most influential female presence in America, but in May of that year, it all came to a watery end, when on her way to swim in the ocean, she disappeared. An extensive search found no body, and it was assumed that the sharks had gotten her. But astonishingly, a month later, she stumbled out of the Sonora Desert with a story of being kidnapped. However, a little poking around by reporters revealed another story—that Aimee had merely shacked up with a boyfriend. Whether the story was true or not, Aimee's popularity took a nosedive, and her grand temple became the object of a tug of war between her mother and her daughter. Another failed marriage put Aimee on a downhill slide, and in 1944, she was found dead beside a bottle of sleeping pills.

WILLIAM SAMUEL STEPHENSON
1897–1989
The Enigma Man

Ian Fleming, author of the famous James Bond spy novels, wrote this about William Stephenson: "James Bond is a highly romanticized version of a true spy. The real thing is William Stephenson."

Born William Samuel Cloustan Stanger in Winnipeg, Manitoba, he was adopted into the Stephenson family when his parents could no longer provide for him. William left school at a young age to work as a telegraph operator, and in 1916, he volunteered for the Canadian Expeditionary Force. In England, he transferred to the Canadian Engineer Corp as a sergeant, and in 1917, gained a commission in the Royal Flying Corps.

Stephenson shot down 12 enemy aircraft, but he was shot down himself in July 1918 and spent the remainder of the war in a concentration camp. Repatriated home with the Military and Distinguished Flying Crosses on his chest, Stephenson immediately jumped into the hardware business, manufacturing a unique German can opener that he had seen his prison

guards use. His business quickly went bust, so Stephenson
returned to England to produce and market small parts for the
manufacture of radios and automobiles. Small parts led to big
parts, and within a few years, Stephenson was a wealthy industrialist with a dreadful secret. A few years into his rise to
industrial greatness, he had come across a wireless message-
sending device whose messages were decipherable only if you
had another machine with the correct rotor setting—a key.
The "secret writing machine" was the brainchild of German
engineer Arthur Scherbius, who invented it at the end of
World War I.

Stephenson's warning to Winston Churchill about the code
machine went nowhere, but in 1936, Stephenson became
privy to information that Adolph Hitler was spending huge

sums on German military buildup in violation of the Treaty of Versailles. Now Churchill listened, and when war broke out over Poland, Stephenson was in New York City setting up the British Security Coordination (BSC), an intelligence agency with an agenda to aid the Allied cause in the Western Hemisphere.

Code named "Intrepid," Stephenson embarked on a campaign to neutralize all the enemy agents in the U.S., either by turning them in or by outright assassination. He helped initiate the U.S. intelligence service, the Office of Strategic Services (OSS), later called the CIA, and to train agents for Europe, he set up Camp X on the shore of Lake Ontario, near Oshawa. He was privy to every secret British and American operation throughout World War II, including the transcripts from the secret writing machine that the Germans called "Enigma." William Stephenson, the man called Intrepid, was Britain's eyes and ears during the entire war and a 100-percent weird and wonderful Canadian.

EDWIN ALONZO BOYD
1914–2002
Canada's Own John Dillinger

Eddie Boyd had a normal upbringing—his father was a Toronto cop, and though Eddie wasn't a great student, he excelled in athletics, especially soccer. He joined the army in 1939, and the next year, he found himself across the pond doing battle for king and country. After six months of fighting, he returned to London, where he met and married a woman named Doreen Thompson. They had a child who unfortunately became a casualty of the Blitz, but the couple would persevere and have three more children.

Back in Toronto after the war and unable to find work to support his wife and children, Eddie Boyd opened his bag of souvenir war pistols, and on September 9, 1949, he robbed the North York branch of the Bank of Montreal of several thousand dollars. Over the next two years, Eddie pulled off perhaps as many as a dozen bank robberies, some with the aid of a partner, Howard Gault. In October 1951, police apprehended Howard, who gave up Eddie to lighten his sentence. In Toronto's Don Jail, Eddie met Lennie and Willie Jackson, and though the two Jacksons were not related, both were experienced bank robbers with a "Get Out of Jail Free" card, a hacksaw blade concealed inside Lennie's wooden foot.

After they broke out of jail on November 4, 1951, the trio joined Cochrane, Ontario, musician-turned-bank-robber Steve Suchan. The newspapers dubbed them the "Boyd Gang," and turned them into folk heroes. That nonsense ended on March 6, 1952, when Lennie and Steve got into a gunfight with Toronto police and killed a detective, an action that resulted in them being wounded and taken into custody. Eddie and Willie were later tracked down during a massive manhunt. On September 8, a few days before Steve and Lennie were to go on trial for murder, the four men escaped from the Don Jail again, though Steve and the two Jacksons were recaptured 10 days later during the biggest manhunt in Ontario's history.

Eddie was cornered and captured on March 15, 1953, in a house at 42 Heath Street West in Toronto. He gave up without a fight but was detained in the house for almost an hour to allow then-mayor Allan Lamport time to arrive and be photographed helping with the arrest. Sentenced to life, Eddie Boyd won parole after a 10-year stretch and lived out his days in British Columbia under an assumed name while driving a bus for handicapped people.

ROBERT "BOB" REGULY
1931–2011
He Informed a Curious Nation

Born in Thunder Bay, Ontario, and knowing that he wanted to be a newspaper reporter from the get-go, Bob Reguly's degree in journalism from the University of Western Ontario got him a job first with the *Sudbury Star*, and then as editor and reporter at small newspapers across the country. His career culminated as an investigative reporter at the *Toronto Star*. He successfully tracked down and interviewed fugitive labour leader Hal Banks, something both the RCMP and the FBI had failed to do, and two years later, in 1966, he broke the most sensational story of the time, the Munsinger Affair.

Montréal playgirl Gerta Munsinger, an East German citizen and suspected Russian spy, had established a prostitute relationship with several Canadian politicians, including Pierre Sevigny, the Associate Defence Minister in John Diefenbaker's government. Munsinger had immigrated to Canada in 1955, and her work as a Montréal nightclub hostess attracted the attention of the FBI, who as early as 1960 had been recording her midnight trysts with politicians. The FBI knew that Gerta was bedding a cabinet minister but were unable to identify the man. They gave the tapes to the RCMP, who knew immediately from the strange thump on every tape that Gerta's conquest was Pierre Sevigny—the thump was the sound of him dropping his wooden leg onto the floor. The political cover-up was quick and absolute—the RCMP picked up Munsinger and deported her back to East Germany, while Sevigny quietly resigned.

That was the end of the story until 1966, when Liberal cabinet minister Lucien Cardin came under attack by conservative MPs in Parliament for the government's handling of a Vancouver mail clerk accused of spying for the Russians. Cardin shouted back to his accusers, "What about Monsignor?" Cardin had gotten the name wrong, but it was enough for the media to break the story—one the government denied—claiming that Gerta Munsinger had died of leukemia in 1964. This sounded contrived to Bob Reguly, who began an extensive hunt for Munsinger, first in East and then in West Germany, where he found her alive and well in Munich. From there, Bob wrote sensational stories that galvanized the public and closed down Parliament for weeks. Munsinger, who freely admitted to bedding not only Sevigny but also several other cabinet ministers, only smiled in response to Bob's questions about being an East German spy.

Bob went on to break more sensational news stories and covered the war in Vietnam, the assassination of Robert Kennedy and the India–Pakistan war, finally becoming the *Star*'s Washington and Ottawa bureau chief.

During the late 1970s, Bob took on an editorial job at the *Toronto Sun*, sharing a byline with reporter Donald Ramsay. In 1981, he failed to check a Ramsay story that accused Northern Development Minister John Munroe of financially benefiting from his office, and Bob's oversight resulted in a huge lawsuit against the paper because the story was a complete fabrication. Bob resigned and began doing public relations for the Ontario government, but you cannot keep a writer down for long and he was soon busy doing articles for outdoor magazines, an endeavour he enjoyed doing until a heart problem turned his attention to his own survival.

WINSTON BLACKMORE
1952–
Our Man of Marital Excess

Why a man would want 26 wives and 100 children is a question that defies logic until the "relative equation" is examined. Winston Blackmore is a former bishop of a breakaway sect of polygamist Mormons who own much of the land around Creston, British Columbia, as well as the sect's headquarters, the town of Bountiful. He has a lot of relatives—nearly all 1000 residents of Bountiful are the descendants of six men, with two being Blackmores.

As anyone who has watched *The Sopranos* on TV knows, family is power, and Winston Blackmore has plenty of family around Creston. He has relatives in local police forces and on the boards of sect-owned companies around the province, businesses that pull in the millions of dollars that the residents of Bountiful spend in Creston. Blackmore is like the king of Bountiful and makes all the decisions for every resident—who will marry whom, who will get an education and who will work where. Brides go to the most faithful, with the not so faithful getting none or the boot.

Polygamy is against the law in Canada, so why is Bountiful still there and growing ever larger? Both the federal and the BC governments have tried to put Blackmore in prison but have been constantly stymied by Canada's constitution, which guarantees freedom of religion, a loophole that Blackmore's lawyer relatives employ like a Monoploy "Get Out of Jail Free" card. Meanwhile, Winston Blackmore, who considers himself above the law, continues his "relative equation."

WILLIAM RUSSELL "BILLY" JAMIESON
1954–2011
Our Indiana Jones

Born in Oakville, Ontario, and knowing from an early age he was destined to be Canada's ethnological gyre, the impatient and ever-curious Billy Jamieson journeyed into the jungles of Ecuador and Peru in 1995 to search for cultural legends—amulets, spears, blow pipes and those ultimate icons of indigenous jungle warfare, shrunken heads. Several more expeditions created a problem for Billy because his treasures were piling up, and he had no place to display or keep them. The problem was compounded in 1996 after he bought the entire collection of Canada's oldest museum, the famed Niagara Falls Museum. Billy's vast collection of ethnographic and archaeological treasures began to really pile up, but building a museum required money, and the Niagara Falls purchase had him eating mac and cheese cooked in the microwave.

He hoped a museum would buy some of his overstock, preferably the four Egyptian mummies from the Niagara's Egyptian collection because Billy feared that their already fragile condition would deteriorate without proper care. He offered the mummies to every museum in Canada, a prerequisite to being able to offer them to U.S. museums—the mummies had been in Canada for so long and were considered so culturally important that our institutions required right of first refusal. Refusals in hand and the phone to his ear, Billy soon interested the Michael C. Carlos Museum in Atlanta, Georgia, into purchasing the mummies. In March 1999, he finally sold them for a sum that allowed him to construct an Art Deco redux of New York's Radio City Music Hall to not only display his beloved treasures, but also to throw the greatest Halloween parties in the known universe, a sample of which can be viewed on YouTube.

Billy passed away in 2011, and though he is truly gone for good, it is nice to think he is just off exploring and will put in an appearance any day now.

DID YOU KNOW?

The Grand Trunk Pacific Railway delivered the first automobile into isolated Jasper Park, Alberta, in the spring of 1914 for the use of a visiting American tourist. A good idea, thought another tourist, as the park had 25 miles (40 kilometres) of interior road and what better way to see the sights, so before summer, another car arrived. However, the sightseers' enjoyment would be short lived, because a few days later, with 25 miles of empty road available for travel, both cars were involved in a head-on collision.

The
Industrialists

The brewers and millers came first because the British
army needed them to supply its soldiers with their daily
bread and a two-litre-per-man beer ration. They were
given free land on which to build breweries, transportation for equipment and a brewing contract, and
over time, men such as Joseph Bloore, John Molson,
Alexander Keith, Thomas Carling and John Labatt
prospered.

The millers, who had grain surpluses to deal with after
Britain repealed the Corn Laws in 1846, became distillers of whisky, and men such as William Gooderham,
Hiram Walker and Joseph Seagram became major
industrialists. Industry needed raw materials—coal
and timber, for example—which in turn stimulated the
transportation industries and fostered the rise of shipping magnates, including Alexander Allan and Samuel
Cunard. However, it would be the railways that set

off massive industrial growth and enticed hundreds of enterprising men to seize the opportunity and become wealthy beyond their wildest dreams.

With no income taxes, whatever money these early industrialists made was all theirs, and being opportunists, most poured it back into other ventures and helped create a great nation from the wilderness. A few such as James Miller Williams and J.H. McKinley were lucky. Williams, already in the business of digging asphalt, struck oil while digging for drinking water—North America's first gusher—and knew how to turn it into gold thanks to Nova Scotia inventor Abraham Gesner's discovery of kerosene. Railway workers J.H. McKinley and Ernest Darragh sought refuge under a lakeside tree during a rainstorm and spotted something shiny in the lake that turned out to be silver—known as the Cobalt silver strike, it was the largest in the world. Whether these men were just lucky or prospered because they had their noses to the grindstone, Canada's weird and wonderful opportunists became the driving force that turned our country into an industrial powerhouse.

THEODORE AUGUST HEINTZMAN
1817–99
Listen to the Music

Theodore Heintzman, a German piano maker, brought his family to New York City from Berlin in 1850, moved to Buffalo, New York, around 1852, and arrived in Toronto some time in 1860 to avoid both the American Civil War and his creditors. He constructed his first small pianos in the back room of his son-in-law's house on Duke Street and later moved operations to a factory at the Junction in 1866. Calling his new enterprise Heintzman & Company, he began the manufacture of grand and player pianos that sold like hotcakes and made Heintzman an extremely wealthy man.

In 1889, he constructed a fine home at the Junction on Annette Street that he called The Birches. The house is still standing today, with a fully renovated exterior along with modern internal modifications wrought by a property developer.

WILLIAM GOODERHAM
1790–1881
Our Original John Barleycorn

In 1837, while experiencing an overstock of grain from bumper crops, flour millers William Gooderham and his brother-in-law and partner James Wort, son of the fantastic windmill builder James Wort Sr., decided to try their hand at distilling the good stuff. The Gooderham and Wort partnership made very good stuff indeed, and though customers had to pay the taxman, the vast quantities that the distillers produced enabled them to offer low prices and turned G&W whisky into an international bargain.

In 1861, the partners built a new distillery, the largest in Canada, with its own wharf on Toronto Bay and a grain silo with a holding capacity of 80,000 bushels (2.8 million litres). It was a strange business for a devout Anglican like Gooderham, who eschewed his own product, but drinking the local water in those days was like playing Russian roulette, with the dreaded cholera always a threat. In essence, Gooderham was doing the public a service by making quality hooch. He would compensate for keeping the town plastered by providing employment for hundreds of Torontonians. Gooderham liked to build things—he rebuilt his distillery using expensive imported stone, a magnificent edifice known today as Toronto's Distillery District, and he constructed neat little homes for his workers, with many still in use today. He also built Little Trinity Church for their Sunday worship.

Bargain-priced, quality whisky made William Gooderham a rich man, but it turned his son and grandson, both named George William, into whisky kings and the richest men in Canada for decades. In 1890, William's first son, George, bought the "Coffin Block" property at the apex of Wellington, Front and Church Streets and constructed Toronto's famous Gooderham Building (also known as the Flatiron Building), an architectural wonder that predated New York City's Flatiron Building by 10 years.

JOHN SULLIVAN DEAS
1838–80
British Columbia's Tin Man

A freeborn black man and experienced tinsmith, John Deas arrived in Victoria, British Columbia, from San Francisco around 1862 and found his skills much in demand. By 1866, he had established Birmingham House, a small manufacturing company that produced stovepipes, store counters and various types of containers made of tin. His containers caught the imagination of Captain Edward Stamp, a wealthy Victoria lumberman on the lookout for a new business venture.

After lumber and gold, cured salmon was British Columbia's main export, but not wanting to get involved in the cumbersome process of barrel salt-curing, Captain Stamp approached John Deas and asked the question that would change the industry: "Can you make tin containers for packing salmon?" Deas' affirmative reply included a demonstration of how quickly he could make a tin can.

In 1871, Captain Stamp bought derelict waterfront buildings in Sapperton, BC, for his Stamp's Fish Preserving Company and put Deas in charge of a crew of Chinese workers making cans. They shipped out 700 cases of 48 one-pound (453-gram) tins the first year and would have tripled production the following year if Captain Stamp had not died from a heart attack. Knowing he was onto a good thing, in 1873, Deas moved his can makers onto an island in the Fraser River (now called Deas Island) south of Vancouver and continued packing salmon. For five years, the Deas Cannery was the largest on the Fraser River, and to the black entrepreneur who employed hundreds of Chinese workers canning fish caught by an ethnically diverse fleet of fishermen, it must have seemed like managing the Tower of Babel.

Deas' success attracted competitors, and by 1878, there were eight canneries on the Fraser River shipping over 100,000 cases of canned fish per year. John Deas realized the dangers of overfishing, and with his pleas to provincial authorities to limit licences ignored, he sold his business and used the proceeds to buy a rooming house.

MAJOR-GENERAL SIR HENRY MILL PELLATT
1859–1939
Our Unfortunate Castle Builder

After graduating from Toronto's Upper Canada College, Henry Pellatt took a job as a clerk in his father's successful investment company, eventually becoming a full partner in 1883. That same year, he bought control of the Toronto Electric Light Company from founder J.J. Wright and invested in Niagara Falls power projects. By 1892, and in full control of his father's firm, Pellatt's speculations turned to railway, bank and land investments that proved so successful that by 1900, he controlled 25 percent of Canada's economy. The high point of Pellatt's life occurred in 1905, when he received a knighthood for his role as commanding officer and chief financial benefactor of the Queen's Own Rifles, a city militia unit.

Pellatt had the golden touch in business, and with so much money rolling in, he decided to make good on a promise to his wife, Lady Mary, to build her a castle, and for that he hired famed Toronto architect E.J. Lennox. Completed in 1914, Casa Loma, the Pellatts' "castle on the hill," was lavishly furnished with French imports, and the conservatory was stocked with rare tropical plants. Lady Mary had her dream home, a real castle with crenellated parapets, towers, 40 servants, 52 telephones, a library with 10,000 books, an elevator and a marvellous view of the city. Only, like all dreams, it did not last because, during World War I, many of Sir Henry's companies were nationalized and he received no financial compensation. After the war, Canada fell into an economic depression and Sir Henry's investments soured. He lost over $2 million when the Home Bank of Canada collapsed, and with money no longer rolling in, Sir Henry lost Casa Loma to the city for back taxes. His wife succumbed to a heart attack in 1924, and Sir Henry's downward spiral continued. In 1929, broke and homeless, he was taken in by his former chauffeur. Sir Henry died in 1939 with $200 in his pocket and owning only the clothes on his back; however, he was not forgotten by the city, as his funeral was the largest ever held in Toronto.

EDWARD SAMUEL "TED" ROGERS
1900–39
Our Wireless Wizard

Born frail, Ted Rogers' parents were told that their son would likely not survive more than a few years, and though Ted did die a young man at age 39, it was enough time for him to become one of Canada's wealthiest citizens through what he called his "tools of success"—hard work and dedication.

Ted aimed that dedication solely at communication, and by 1911, he had one of the first shortwave radio licences in Canada. In fact, he was the first in Toronto to hear reports of the *Titanic* sinking in 1912 and posted that information at city bus stops. He did the same in 1914 when World War I was declared. In 1921, he became the first Canadian wireless operator to send a message to Europe, a feat that earned him the title of "Wireless Wizard." Three years later, while on a visit to the U.S., he happened to see a demonstration of a new type of radio vacuum tube and immediately got a licence for Canada, and in 1925, he improved on the AC radio tube and began to manufacture and distribute lightweight radios. He founded the iconic CFRB radio station in 1927.

Ted and his wife, Velma, welcomed a son, Edward Samuel "Ted" Rogers Jr., in 1933, and, following in his father's footsteps, the boy grew up to be the master of Canada's airwaves.

EDWARD PLUNKET "E.P." TAYLOR
1901–89
Sunshine in a Cup

Born in Ottawa, Ontario, Edward Taylor graduated from McGill University in 1922 and then went on to parlay his family's beer business into an industrial empire that included the Brewing Corporation of Ontario (now Canadian Breweries Ltd.) and Argus Corporation. He went on to either control or hold significant positions on the boards of many of the country's largest corporations, including Massey-Harris, Orange Crush Ltd., Canadian Food Products, Standard Chemical, Dominion Tar & Chemical Company, Dominion Stores, Standard Broadcasting and Hollinger Mines Ltd. At the peak of his career, he was one of Canada's richest businessmen. However, Taylor is best known to Torontonians for his Windfields Farm racehorse-breeding endeavour, which provided Canada with the king of racehorses, Northern Dancer.

Although not a native Torontonian, Taylor qualifies as a favourite son because his principle residence during his most successful years was Windfields Estate at 2489 Bayview Avenue, now operated as the Canadian Film Centre. During the early 1960s, Taylor constructed the Lyford Quay housing and golf course project in the Bahamas and retired to that epitome of gracious living. But in 1973, he came out of retirement to take over International Housing Ltd., and by 1978, he was building low-cost housing in 40 countries around the world.

Taylor passed away in 1989 at the age of 88 in Lyford Quay in the Bahamas. On that day, shoppers at Toronto's Simpsons store crowded around the store's Honeydew stand and toasted his accomplishments with the orange drink made ubiquitous by Taylor. Of all his business undertakings, E.P. got the biggest kick out of Honeydew, and as one of only three people who knew the formula for mixing the beverage's base, he seldom missed an opportunity to don a white coat and help with the mixing.

Our
Inventors

Canadians have patented more than one million inventions, and yet very few people can name even three or four of the weird and wonderful men and women who have improved our lives through countless hours of thought and tinkering. So few Canadians are cognizant of the nation's contributions to world betterment that Alexander Graham Bell's name is bantered about like a talisman against national ineptitude. The truth is, Bell did not actually invent the telephone—he perfected the device, and in Canada, he simply tried it out. And the famous "Wizard of Menlo Park," Thomas Edison, is credited with inventing the electric light bulb, when, in fact, he merely perfected an invention patented by Henry Woodward of Toronto. Peanut butter, one of the most iconic American foods, was invented in 1884 by Montréal resident Marcellus Gilmore Edson. Two years later, Thomas Ahearn from Ottawa invented the electric cooking range, the electric

iron and heaters for streetcars and automobiles. The green ink in U.S. currency was a 1862 invention by Thomas Sterry Hunt, a Canadian. Pemmican, a nutritious mix of pounded meat, fat and berries invented by Canadian First Nations tribes, was the convenience food that enabled the fur trade and the exploration of Canada. Ontario farmer David Fife hybridized a strain of wheat that turned empty prairie land into one of the world's great breadbaskets, while John McIntosh gave the world his famous red apple. The list of life-bettering Canadian inventions is long and varied, and while some of the inventors were bewhiskered old cranks, many were weird, wild and wonderful individuals deserving of a mention.

ABRAHAM PINEO GESNER
1797–1864
The Lamplighter Who Saved the Whales

Born in Nova Scotia's Annapolis Valley, Abraham Pineo Gesner took to the sea as a lad, but after two disastrous shipwrecks, he wisely decided to pursue a career in medicine. In London, England, he learned the art of healing and picked up an interest in geology, a science he would actively pursue, and in 1836, he published a survey of Nova Scotia's iron ore and coal deposits.

Coal intrigued Gesner, and he was often found covered head to toe in coal dust. In 1838, when he was appointed provincial geologist for New Brunswick, he began experimenting in earnest with coal and another mineral called albertite, a bituminous asphalt. In 1846, after several explosive failures, his experiments paid off with a distilled substance he called "kerosene." It burned cleaner and brighter and was much cheaper than any competing product, the most important being whale oil.

In 1850, Gesner began producing kerosene commercially. Calling his endeavour the Kerosene Gaslight Company, he began lighting up the streets of Halifax and other Maritime cities. By 1854, he had expanded his business into the U.S. as the North American Gaslight Company and was distilling purely from coal, a process that earned his product the nickname "coal oil." Standard Oil eventually bought Gesner's company, allowing him to retire a very rich man. Gesner was the Canadian who lit up the world and saved the whales from being rendered into extinction.

DANIEL DAVID "D.D." PALMER
1835–1913
The First Chiropractor

Born in Pickering, Ontario, Daniel Palmer developed an interest in magnetic healing early on. In 1855, during a period of economic depression, he moved with his family to Davenport, Iowa, where he clerked in a grocery store and worked part time as a beekeeper. All the while, he continued to pursue his interest in magnetic healing, an interest he finally made professional by opening an office for the treatment of patients.

Not long after he began his practice, Palmer encountered the building's deaf janitor, Harvey Lillard, and learned that his deafness was the result of a lifting accident. Palmer found a lump on Lillard's spine, theorized that the man had popped a vertebra, and after a bit of bone manipulation, succeeded in restoring Lillard's hearing.

In 1897, Palmer founded the first school of chiropractic medicine and immediately began spending much time in courts and various jails for practising medicine without a licence. After one 17-day stretch in prison, he called it quits and sold the school to his son, B.J. Palmer, but could never stop meddling in school affairs. This created such hostility between the pair that rumour claimed the son ran over his father with a motorcar and realigned his bones permanently.

JOHN J. WRIGHT
1847–1922
The Man Who Put the Zap in Streetcars

John J. Wright's first effort to move a railcar by electric motor was a bust—at a demonstration in front of thousands of spectators at the Canadian National Exhibition (CNE), the car refused to budge more than a few feet. The crowd laughed, booed and pointed fingers, but undaunted, Wright returned to the drawing board, and his demonstration at the 1884 CNE was better but still unimpressive.

In 1885, Wright was back, having invented a new way to supply electricity to the railcar's motor through an overhead wire with a pole connection. His electrified streetcar worked like a dream and hauled over 50,000 CNE patrons, including the Warren brothers, Toronto's public transportation moguls. By 1890, people attending the CNE could arrive there using a Warren brothers' Toronto Street Railway Company electrified streetcar from almost anywhere in the city.

THOMAS AHEARN
1855–1938
He Plugged Us into the Electrical Age

Born in Ottawa, Ontario, Thomas Ahearn knew from an early age that electricity was the way of the future, and at age 15, he presented himself to the J.R. Booth Company, a Ottawa telegraph operator, offering to work for free in exchange for learning telegraphy. From there, he moved on to manage a local Bell Telephone exchange, and in 1882, he formed his own electrical contracting company, Ahern & Soper. He set up telephones for Canada's Parliament Buildings and illuminated the city with 165 arc lamps.

Ahern was a man possessed of amazing energy and curiosity, and while other men slept, he tinkered with electricity. In 1882, he invented the electric cooking range and cooked his dinner with electricity, but it took him another decade to perfect the electric oven, the first of which was installed at Ottawa's Windsor Hotel. In 1887, Ahern lit up Parliament Hill with a 1000 light bulbs for Queen Victoria's Jubilee celebration, and his company installed the first coast-to-coast telegraph system. In 1891, he put electric streetcars on the streets of Ottawa and started a company to manufacture the streetcars.

Already a wealthy man, Ahearn could have rested on his laurels, but he kept inventing and gave Canadians the first car heater, electric water heater and flatiron. Thomas Ahearn, was a weird, wild and wonderful Canadian inventor who made our lives better through electricity.

JOHN J. McLAUGHLIN
1865–1914
He Made Canada as Dry as Champagne

In 1890, John McLaughlin, an Enniskillon, Ontario, pharmacist and the eldest son of Oshawa, Ontario, carriage maker Robert McLaughlin, opened a seltzer plant in Toronto. Making ginger beer seemed like a natural progression, but everyone made ginger beer, so he took another path and invented a crisper, drier, less sweet product he called McLaughlin's Belfast Style Ginger Ale. A patented product sold in bottles, the drink became a favourite of the Duke of Devonshire, who called it "the champagne of ginger ales," a slogan eventually used on both the label and in advertising. At its inception, McLaughlin's bottle label featured a picture of a beaver superimposed over a map of Canada, for which he received some criticism from the government in Ottawa, so he substituted a crown for the beaver.

John J. died in 1914, so his brother, the Oshawa carmaker Colonel "Sam" McLaughlin, took over the company's operations until he sold out in 1923. At the onset of U.S. Prohibition, whenever Colonel Sam visited Detroit to discuss car making with General Motors, board members demanded that he bring along a supply of his Canadian dry ginger ale, a service that probably helped his business and prompted the new owners of the beverage company to assume the name Canada Dry. During Prohibition, John McLaughlin's weird and wonderful beverage was already being manufactured in New York City and caught on like wildfire because it easily masked the flavour of bathtub gin.

REGINALD AUBREY FESSENDEN
1866–1932
The Man Who Took the Buzz Out of Radio

Today, radio entertainment is as common as air, but before Christmas Eve 1906, when Canadian Reginald Fessenden leaned into his microphone and sang "O Holy Night," it was nonexistent. Born in East Bolton, Québec, and educated at Bishop's University in Lennoxville, Fessenden left school before graduating and travelled to New Jersey to learn about electricity from Thomas Edison. While he was there, he invented the nickel-iron leads for the light bulb.

Laid off when Edison encountered financial trouble, Fessenden went to work for George Westinghouse, and by 1898, he had created a working wireless communication system between the cities of Pittsburgh and Allegany. In 1900, he got a job with the U.S. Weather Bureau, and on December 23 of that year, he made the first wireless audio transmission over a distance of 1.6 miles (2.5 kilometres). Although he worked mostly in the U.S., Fessenden still found time to work in Canada, and in 1904, he helped engineer the power plant at Niagara Falls for the Hydro-Electric Power Commission of Ontario. During World War I, he volunteered his services to the Canadian government and was sent to London, England, where he developed devices to locate enemy artillery and sonar to find submarines. In 1915, he invented the fathometer, a sonar device for measuring sea depth, and in later years, he developed tracer bullets, marine turbine engines, an advanced television and about 500 other inventions. Fessenden never slaved in a stuffy laboratory—he got his ideas while smoking a cigar and lying on his back, sometimes in a swimming pool and sometimes on the floor with his cat.

An inventor is one who can see the applicability of means of supplying demand five years before it is obvious to those skilled in the art.

–Reginald A. Fessenden, inventor

WILLIAM WALLACE GIBSON
1876–1965
Our All-Canadian Birdman

On February 23, 1909, the Graham Bell–sponsored *Silver Dart* took to the air, becoming the first powered aircraft to fly in the British Commonwealth, but though the *Dart* was a success for Canada, it was not an all-Canadian aircraft. Its design was a Canadian–American collaboration powered by an all-American Curtis V8 automobile engine. The first all-Canadian airplane, including the engine, was designed, constructed and flown on September 10, 1910, by Victoria, BC, resident William Wallace Gibson.

Gibson's planes were little more than kites, but the engine was a remarkable piece of engineering that weighed half as much as the Curtis V8 and produced five additional horsepower with half the number of cylinders. Gibson had made a fortune in BC gold mining and spent it all perfecting the first Canadian aircraft engine, for which he earned little or no credit.

DONALD LEWIS HINGS
1907–2004
The Man Who Gave a Voice to War

Donald Hings arrived in Canada from England in 1907 with his mother, going first to Lethbridge, Alberta, and then to Vancouver. Hings' formal education ended at middle school because of financial difficulties, but Vancouver had a good library, and he educated himself there, developing an interest in wireless communications. In the mid-1920s, while working at part-time jobs, Hings took a two-year wireless course that would eventually land him a job with the Consolidated Mining and Smelting Company (Cominco) in 1930.

The company had a problem communicating with its geologists in the field, one that Hings eventually solved by inventing a portable wireless device that he called the Backset. Cominco liked it so much that they set Hings up in a laboratory to perfect the device and even allowed him to keep the patents. Hings was happy at Cominco, but when war broke out in 1938, he beat a path to Ottawa and so impressed military officials that they, too, set up him in a laboratory. He was given the temporary rank of general and ran around battlefields demonstrating and testing his as-yet-unnamed portable communication device. In fact, his invention was christened on a battlefield when a newspaper reporter asked a soldier using the device what it did. The soldier replied, "You can walk with it while you talk," and that reporter wrote down the immortal words "walkie-talkie."

Donald Hings' walkie-talkie, a device created by the mind of a truly great inventor, probably shortened the war and saved many lives.

JOHN L. EDLUND
1873–1957
Saving Lives with a Suitcase

After surviving three ship sinkings, John Edlund emigrated from Norway to Claresholm, Alberta, in 1904, where his experiences at sea prompted his invention of the lifesaving flotation suitcase in the 1920s. The suitcase converted into a buoyant, full-body, rubber suit. Weighing only 12 pounds (5.4 kilograms), the suit could keep a person dry and safe for up to four days in rough seas. The invention went nowhere until the 1990s, when it re-emerged as a good idea.

JOSEPH L. COYLE
1872–1972
Our Egg-straordinary Inventor

In 1911, Joseph Coyle, the publisher of the *Interior News* newspaper in Smithers, British Columbia, stopped an argument between a farmer and a hotel owner. The farmer shipped eggs to a hotel, but the eggs often arrived broken, angering the hotel owner. Coyle solved the problem by inventing the paper egg carton, which he called the "Egg-Safety Carton." Later, he invented a machine to make the egg cartons and moved to Vancouver to manufacture and license others to produce millions of cartons.

A lifelong inventor, Coyle also developed a wool-carding machine, a boat propelled by bicycle pedals, a match dispenser, a fruit box and a coin-sorting machine.

CHARLES HENRY COLL
1907–82
The Greatest Invention Since Sliced Bread

Born in Stellarton, Nova Scotia, avid outdoorsman Charles Coll got his start inventing animal and fish lures, and he patented the name "Muskol Lures" in 1959. In the early 1960s, his experiments led to the development of the legendary insect repellent, Muskol. The name Muskol is a play on the words "musk," a deer's scent, "call," which means to entice or lure, and Charles' surname, Coll.

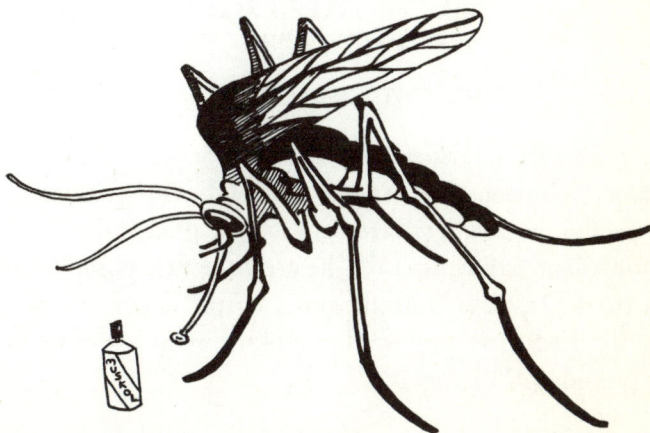

ROBERT "ROMAN" GONSETT
1891–1951
He Invented the Answering Machine

Born in the Ukraine, Roman Gonsett immigrated to Calgary, Alberta, in 1907, where he set up a laboratory and began inventing electronic devices. He created the telephone answering machine and the whimsical Fairy Phonograph, a combination of Edison's phonograph and a lamp.

In 1916, Gonsett moved his family to Burbank, California, and established the Gonset Company, which manufactured electronic equipment. Although the Gonsetts remained in the U.S., they never forgot their time in Canada, and in 1956, Roman's wife and son donated $1000 to the University of Alberta to establish the R.R. Gonsett Memorial Ukrainian Library.

HOWARD DILL
1935–2008
Our Own Great Pumpkin

During the 1960s, farmer and self-taught geneticist Howard Dill from Windsor, Nova Scotia, started the international giant pumpkin-growing craze with his patented "Dill's Atlantic Giant" seeds. In 1979, he grew the first pumpkin to break the 400-pound (180-kilogram) barrier, and in modern times, his seeds have produced pumpkins weighing more than 1600 pounds (725 kilograms).

To honour its native son, in 1984, Windsor held its first Pumpkin Regatta, and every year since then, local residents have hollowed out pumpkin shells and raced them across nearby Lake Pesaquid.

RACHEL ZIMMERMAN
1972–
The Girl Who Spoke in Symbols

In 1984, at the age of only 12, Rachel Zimmerman of London, Ontario, introduced the world to her Blissymbol printer at her school's science fair. Her invention, a computer program that allows severely disabled people to tap symbols on a keyboard for translation onto a screen, enables non-speaking individuals to "talk." The device won her many awards, including the silver medal at the World Exhibition of Achievement of Young Inventors. She completed her college degree in physics and space in 1990, and eventually landed a job with NASA's Jet Propulsion Laboratory in Pasadena, California.

BORN IN CANADA NOBEL PRIZE RECIPIENTS
Our Brainiacs

☛ Frederick Grant Banting, 1923, for the co-discovery of insulin

☛ David H. Hubel, 1981, for co-discovering processes in the human visual system

☛ Henry Taube, 1983, for his work on electron transfer mechanisms

☛ Sidney Altman, 1989, for the co-discovery of the catalytic properties of RNA

☛ Richard E. Taylor, 1990, for his work in particle physics

☛ Rudolph M. Marcus, 1992, for his work on electron transfer in chemical systems

- Bertram N. Brockhouse, 1994, for co-pioneering the study of condensed matter

- Willard. S. Boyle, 2009, for his co-invention of an imaging semiconductor circuit

DID YOU KNOW?

Considering the threats from birds and birdbrains, being the world's largest producer of icewine is an amazing achievement for Canada. In 1982, only the most adventurous vintners were leaving grapes to dry in the winter cold. Walter Strehn of Ontario's Pelee Island Winery was one of those, and to keep birds from consuming his crop, he placed a net over his acreage. That worked until a few blue jays managed to muscle in and get Walter reported to the Ministry of Natural Resources by an outraged birdwatcher. MNR agents tore down the net, allowing the birds to polish off the crop and charged Walter with trapping birds without a licence.

Our
Mariners

*Before Canada became a nation, it was a loose con-
federation of seaports. During the country's formative
years, most Canadians lived in Maritime seaports
and made their living either directly or indirectly
from the sea. Ships transported raw materials, furs
and salted fish out, and returned with goods from
abroad. They also brought the lifeblood of the new
nation—people—the thousands of immigrants who
would fan out into the wilderness and make it produc-
tive. Canada owes its all to the sea and to the weird,
wild, and wonderful men and women who sailed its
dangerous waters.*

ENOS COLLINS
1774–1871
Merchant, Pirate and Canadian Banker

Born in Massachusetts, Enos Collins came to Liverpool, Nova Scotia, with his merchant trader family and hit the bounding main as a cabin boy, travelling back and forth to the Caribbean on his family's ships. By his teens, he was an experienced sea captain intent on some adventure for profit—privateering.

In 1799, Collins served as a ship's officer aboard the Liverpool-investor-financed, 16-gun *Charles Mary Wentworth*, the most feared privateer of her day, and within two years, he had enough prize money to construct an even more fearsome vessel, the *Liverpool Packet*. Yo, ho, ho and a bottle of rum, and in no time at all, young Collins had the wherewithal and enough ships to move to Halifax. In 1811, he bought the wharf and warehouses of that city's main merchant, Charles Prescott, who had just retired.

While the War of 1812 raged, Collins kept his ships busy hauling fish and lumber to the West Indies, returning with rum and supplies for the British military while the *Liverpool Packet* prowled for prizes. In 1822, he became a member of "His Majesties Council," which, along with an assembly, was the governing body of Nova Scotia. Three years later, needing a place to keep all his money, he partnered with friends to open the Halifax Banking Company, precursor to the Imperial Bank of Commerce. In 1826, the Council levied a tax on imported brandy, and in 1830, Collins and Company petitioned the legislative assembly of Halifax for a refund since they were paying the tax in pirated Spanish doubloons and not receiving a proper exchange rate. From the petition, the assembly determined that tax collectors had been undercharging, and they drew up a change to the existing tax laws.

But Collins and the Council refused to accept it, and the tax
was disallowed completely. As luck would have it, Collins had
a huge warehouse stuffed with imported brandy that he
promptly sold tax free. This did not endear him to political
circles, so at age 51, Collins decided to retire and find himself
a wife. He and his new wife, Margaret, had nine kids and
lived the good life in a grand mansion with fantastic gardens
and plenty of servants. And why not? Collins was truly
a weird and wonderful guy and the richest man in Canada
until his death.

SAMUEL CUNARD
1787–1865
Canada's King of Steam

When the Cunard family arrived in Halifax, Nova Scotia,
from the U.S. as United Empire Loyalists, they had almost
nothing but the clothes on their backs. However, the elder
Cunard knew carpentry and soon had the family back on
track by working for the British navy and investing in timber
rights. His son, Samuel, a chip off the old block when it came
to hard work and ambition, was running his own general store
by his 17th birthday and slowly expanding into timber with
his father. The father-and-son team then went into coal, iron,
whaling, shipping and the odd bit of privateering.

Samuel Cunard outfitted his first whaling ship with cannons,
allowing its captain to seize a few vessels as prizes during the
War of 1812, a war in which Cunard served as a captain of
militia. But it was to steam that Cunard hooked his future,
and after co-founding the Steamship Ferry Company in
Halifax, he travelled to England to solicit the mail contract,
promising that his steamships could deliver in half the time
of sailing ships. That contract allowed him to construct the

Britannia, the first steamship with the designation RMS, which stood for "Royal Mail Ship."

In 1840, the RMS *Britannia* steamed from Liverpool to Halifax and on to Boston with Samuel Cunard and 63 passengers aboard. He stressed safety on his ships, and the Cunard Lines maintained a sterling reputation, allowing the company to succeed where others failed. In 1859, Cunard's tenacious adherence to safety regulations and time schedules earned him the title of Baron Cunard from Queen Victoria, an award that he would repay by naming a future ship after the monarch.

After the *Titanic* disaster in 1912, Cunard merged with the owners of the ill-fated ship, the White Star Line, to become the major Atlantic carrier of the 20th century. The company owned dozens of freighters and luxury ships, including the RMS *Queen Victoria* and, in 1936, the venerable *Queen Mary*.

Cunard's ships needed huge amounts of lumber to outfit their luxury interiors and coal for power, and Cunard supplied them both through subsidiary companies. He acquired his coal mines from the Rundle brothers, the king's jewellers, who had bought mineral rights in Nova Scotia from the king so he could pay his son's gambling debts. Cunard heard this on a visit to England, and figuring that the jewellers probably also had gambling debts and needed money, he simply walked into their shop and asked if they wanted to sell—and they did, happily.

Shrewd, ambitious, a stickler for time and safety, and a bit of a pirate, Samuel Cunard is still remembered in the Maritimes as a weird, wild and wonderful Canadian who knew the value of a Spanish doubloon and good head of steam.

JOSHUA SLOCUM
1844–1909
Our Lonely Man of the Sea

He couldn't swim, not one stroke, but the Nova Scotia–born Joshua Slocum did the improbable, single-handedly circum-navigating the world between 1885 and 1889 using only a beat-up clock to determine longitude and noonday sun sight-ings for latitude. He wrote a book detailing his adventures, *Sailing Alone Around the World*, and it made him such a celeb-rity that, in 1901, he and his sailboat *Spray* were invited to appear at the Pan American Exposition in Buffalo, New York.

As a star of that exposition, he was filmed by Thomas Edison, hobnobbed with Buffalo Bill Cody and entertained U.S. presi-dent William McKinley on the *Spray* just a few hours before McKinley was shot to death by an anarchist. Slocum attended the swearing-in ceremony for the new president, Theodore Roosevelt, and the pair became good friends. After the Buffalo exposition, Slocum sailed back down the Erie Canal and then to Martha's Vineyard, where he traded in the sea for a hops farm.

During one of Slocum's visits to Teddy Roosevelt at the White House, he told the president that the farmer's life was not for him and he intended to sail down to Venezuela, travel up the Orinoco River and write another book. In 1909, Slocum sold his farm, sailed off in the *Spray* and disappeared. The consen-sus is that he was run down by a steamboat during the night. Or perhaps he simply forgot about the Orinoco and decided to attempt another circumnavigation.

The world will probably never know the fate of Joshua Slocum, but it will not soon forget him, as there are monu-ments, rivers, flora and a host of ships and boats named for the weird, wild and wonderful Canadian who dared the fantastic and made history.

ANGUS WALTERS
1881–1968
Hard to the Wind and on Every Dime

Born a Lunenburg "Bluenoser," Angus Walters had made
a name for himself as a schooner captain long before the 1919
inception of the great International Fisherman's Trophy Race.
Thought a cinch to win and already well ahead of the competition, Captain Walters loaded on too much sail and snapped
a mainmast, losing what, for the time, was $1 million in
wagers made by his fellow Lunenburgers. Irked and determined to set things right, Walters signed on with a group of
Halifax businessmen to build a redeemer, a schooner to beat
all schooners that they would call the *Bluenose*.

At that time, Canadians were desperate for a hero figure;
World War I and rationing had caused great hardship, jobs
were scarce, police were corrupt and prohibitionists, communists and union sympathizers marched in the streets.
Canadians found their hero in Angus Walters, and when the
day of the big race arrived, almost every ear in the nation was
glued to a radio.

"Our" ship won and was victorious again the next year, but
in 1923, Angus and the *Bluenose* faced their greatest competition, a specially constructed U.S. racing schooner called the
Columbia. Now that it was a real race, every factory, school
and home radio was tuned in when the *Bluenose* won the first
heat, lost the second and won the final. Captain Walters and
Canada's hero ship had triumphed again, but then came the
unbelievable news that the *Bluenose* had been disqualified
because of a rule change. Canadians were devastated until they
found out that the *Columbia*'s crew had refused to accept
a win by a technicality, and to all Canadians, the great ship
Bluenose was still the fastest sailing ship the world had ever

seen. There would not be another Fisherman's Trophy race for eight years, not until 1931, when the *Bluenose* once again claimed the award for Canada.

The fact that the great ship ended her days as a Caribbean work scow tweaked the national consciousness, so in 1969, a keel was laid for another go around—the *Bluenose II*. Today, she sails both on Canadian dimes and from the port of Lunenburg, an icon of the days of sail and the courageous men who put their lives on the line to harvest the bounty of the Grand Banks.

PAMELA DENISE ANDERSON
1967–
Our Sensational Beach Babe

Although she's not a mariner in the traditional sense, Pamela Anderson's surf time on the *Baywatch* TV series more than qualifies her to be Canada's all-time best marine export. Born in Ladysmith, British Columbia, and discovered at a BC Lions football game when her T-shirt-clad image was flashed onto the stadium's big screen, her first steps to fame included a series of beer commercials and the pages of *Playboy* magazine.

In 1990, Pamela moved to Los Angeles to appear in the hit TV series *Home Improvement*, and that led to her most famous role as C.J. Parker on *Baywatch*. A treat for the eyes, but not the sharpest knife in the drawer, she married Mötley Crüe drummer Tommy Lee, divorced him, dated him, dumped him for singer Kid Rock, and then got back together with Lee when she discovered the pair really did have something in common—hepatitis C from a needle they had shared while getting tattoos.

Pamela Anderson is our weird and wonderful babe of the sea, and she still looks scrumptious enough to reprise her C.J. Parker role in any *Baywatch* remake.

The
Agrarians

Newly discovered Canada was a land of immense opportunities—all a person had to do was figure out a way to capitalize on them. With no roads, millions of mosquitoes and black flies and the foulest weather imaginable, taking advantage of those opportunities was a monumental task, and for centuries, opportunists were pretty much confined to chewing away at the edges of the country. Then along came the railway and everything changed; the opportunists followed the tracks inland like mice after the Pied Piper.

The railways spawned settlements and from those extended roadways, allowing the opportunists to find more and varied natural resources and to settle even farther inland. Tracks, roads and the opportunists built this country inward from the edges. The original opportunists, the entrepreneurial lumber barons, miners, ranchers and farmers, have been for the most part

replaced by giant corporate entities because, in a country the size of Canada, big is best when it comes to harvesting natural resources.

That small is not so good was a lesson learned by over 30,000 western settlers who claimed their 160 acres (65 hectares) of "free" prairie land only to become the serfs of Ottawa politicians, the railways and shady government homestead inspectors. The countless small lumber concerns that sprang up in the wilds fared no better because their timber production depended upon greasing the palms of politicians and the vagaries of the railways. Ottawa-appointed registrars often cheated Canadian miners out of their claims, and if railway tracks were not a stone's throw away from their discovery, they had little chance of developing their claims no matter how promising they were.

Canada needed big business to develop, but it did so at the expense of small business. However, this country is so large and now so interconnected by transportation infrastructure that opportunity is back and is knocking almost everywhere.

PETER AYLEN
1799–1868
The King of the Shiners

They called him the "King of the Shiners," the shiners being the private army of Protestant Irish immigrants that Peter Aylen employed to monopolize the timber tracts of the Ottawa Valley. In 1815, working as an apprentice sailor, Aylen jumped ship in Québec City and went to work cutting timber in the Ottawa Valley. Within two decades, he controlled huge tracts through his association with the Gatineau Privilege, a group of politically connected British intent on creating a monopoly to thwart French Canadian lumber interests.

To this end, Aylen hired 200-plus Irish labourers from the just-completed Rideau Canal project and taught them lumbering. They called themselves "Shiners" because they were always covered in sweat and appeared shiny, and to insure loyalty, Aylen supplied his men with rum and prostitutes imported from Montréal. They were his private army, and beginning in 1835, Aylen used them to smash competitors' camps, disrupt their lumber rafting and commit general terrorism. The conflict culminated in what historians call the "Shiners War," an all-out free-for-all between the French lumbermen and Aylen's Irish thugs, with the Irish gaining the upper hand. The Shiners controlled the Bytown (Ottawa) bridge, and with the local constabulary too afraid to intervene, they were free to block Aylen's competitors lumber rafts or charge them a huge toll.

In 1835, Aylen was arrested in Bytown for assaulting a lawyer from Perth, and his Shiners went on a bloody rampage that completely terrorized the town. Vigilante groups were formed that finally put an end to the Shiners, with Aylen fleeing Bytown for Aylmer, Québec. In Aylmer, he settled down with his ill-gotten gains to become a law-abiding citizen. He was so law abiding that in 1848, he was appointed a justice of the peace.

LYDIA CHASE RANNEY
1800–1901
She Put the Word "Big" into Canadian Cheese

After arriving at Salford, in Oxford County, Ontario, from Vermont in about 1830, Lydia taught school while her husband Hiram worked their small farm. Back in Vermont, Lydia had made cheddar cheese, and she quickly talked Hiram into purchasing a few good milk cows. From their milk, she began producing quality cheddar.

Lydia, with an eye to merchandising, produced giant wheels of cheddar that she carted around to agricultural exhibitions to promote her product. After 20 years, Lydia and Hiram were milking over 100 cows and producing tonnes of cheese, and she decided to produce a really big cheese to advertise the business. She and Hiram got to work and created the "Big Cheese," a 1200-pound (544-kilogram) giant wheel of cheddar that the provincial government sent to the Great Exhibition of 1851 in London, England. The event excited both the public and dairymen, and soon Canada had hundreds of cheese factories, with many situated in Oxford County.

In 1893, in a move to emulate Lydia's success, dairymen from around Perth, Ontario, pooled their resources to create another promotional cheese, the "Canadian Mite," a 22,000-pound (9980-kilogram) monster cheddar destined for display at the World's Columbian Exposition in Chicago. Loaded onto a railcar, the behemoth cheese wheel had people lining the tracks for a peek, and while on display in Chicago, it garnered massive crowds and much publicity after it crashed through the floor of the exhibition hall. Back on a railcar, the great cheese was paraded through towns and villages all the way to the east coast. In Halifax, after much ceremony, the mammoth cheddar was loaded onto a ship for a tour of the UK, where after much hoopla, it was cut up and sold.

DAVID ALEXANDER FIFE
1805–77
He Gave Us Our Daily Bread

The Fife family arrived in Otonabee, Upper Canada (near present-day Peterborough, Ontario), from Scotland in 1820 to farm a variety of wheat known as Siberian wheat. It fared pretty badly because the climate made it susceptible to a fungus disease called rust, so the Fifes grew mostly barley and rye. However, one member of the clan, young David Fife, continued to plant the Siberian wheat variety in a small plot in the hope of hybridizing a rust-resistant plant.

In 1825, David married Jane Beckett, a local standout, and shortly afterward, they moved down the road to establish their own farm, and, of course, another experimental plot. Season after season, David got nowhere—his wheat would just rust up and either die or produce withered stalks of grain. In early 1842, he decided to forego his attempts to hybridize Siberian wheat and try another variety. No other wheat variety was available, so David wrote to an old chum in Edinburgh, Scotland, asking for whatever wheat was available there. Probably a no more propitious letter has ever been received because, as David's friend read the letter, a grain ship from Danzig, Prussia, was docking at the harbour. Down to the port went the friend, and into an envelope went a handful of seed grain scrounged off the dock.

When David received the envelope, it had the word *Halychanka* scrawled on the back, and not sure if the variety was winter or spring wheat, he popped some of the seeds into the ground, only to find that it was winter wheat and it failed to ripen. Undaunted, he planted the remainder in the fall, only to have all but three ears of grain eaten by his cow. Come spring, he remembered the three saved ears and planted them in his experimental plot. The seeds grew well, but most succumbed to the ever-present rust disease before harvest. Saving the seeds that survived the rust, David planted them, and the next fall, he was rewarded with his miracle—the wheat stalks in his plot grew faster, taller and stronger than any of his regular Siberian wheat variety and, even better, showed no signs of rust. He immediately planted his entire crop with the new seed, and the following autumn, he reaped a bumper harvest with enough to share his good fortune with neighbours. They called their own bumper crops of rust-free wheat "Red Fife" after the grain's red colour and the weird, wonderful and persistent miracle worker from Otonabee.

MATTHEW HENRY COCHRANE
1823–1903
Our First King of Cattle

Born in Compton County, Lower Canada, Matthew Cochrane travelled to Boston as a young man. There he opened a successful leather goods and shoe company, a business that continued to prosper after he moved to Montréal in 1864.

Prosperity enabled Cochrane to branch into the raising of pedigreed shorthorn cattle, an endeavour he loved and one that brought him international fame as a breeder. In 1872, he became a senator and sat in Parliament, where he used his wit and wiles to push through the federal land-grazing act that allowed for the leasing of huge tracts of western land to folks wanting to raise cattle. Not surprisingly, Cochrane was one of those folks, and he immediately leased the best land for

himself—several huge tracts along the Bow River. It wasn't very ethical, but, hey, Alberta was empty and needed filling, and fill it he did, bringing thousands of head of cattle from Montana in 1881 and '82, about the same time that Fred Stimson was bringing up his herds.

In 1883, Senator Cochrane leased a further 67,000 acres (27,000 hectares) between the Belly and Kootenai Rivers, bringing his total acreage to 334,500 acres (135,400 hectares). Big-time rancher Senator Cochrane loved nothing better than to ride the whole 45-kilometre length of his ranch, surveying his herds, which numbered anywhere from 15,000 to 20,000 animals.

Cochrane died in 1902, and in 1905, his son Billy sold the ranch to the Mormon Church to be subdivided into small farms. To memorialize the days of big cattle ranches, the Alberta government has rebuilt the senator's luxurious 20,000-square-foot (1800-square-metre) ranch house. It's a wonderful stop for tourists and a great day trip for Albertans wanting to see how the senator lived while overseeing Canada's biggest ranch.

FREDERICK STIMSON
1842–1912
Our Second King of Cattle

Born in Compton County in the Eastern Townships of Québec, Fred Stimson took over the family farm when his father passed away, and by 1871, he had built it into the largest in the area. In 1881, in response to a federal government lease initiative, Fred's brother quit the North-West Mounted Police to become a full-time rancher in Alberta, and deciding that ranching was also the life for him, Fred sold the farm and

174

partnered with several wealthy associates to form the North West Cattle Company.

Stimson leased some 50,000 acres (20,000 hectares) centred on Pekisko Creek. He called his ranch the Bar U and brought in 3000 head of cattle from the U.S. along with foremen to oversee the local cowboys. The devastating winter of 1882–83 wiped out several adjoining ranches, but judicious stock management allowed the Bar U to come through relatively unscathed. Stimson was able to buy out leases from the failed ranches and range more cattle. In 1884, the Bar U was selling beef to the Department of Indian Affairs, the North-West Mounted Police and railway contractors, and was shipping live range cattle to Britain. By 1890, Fred Stimson's Bar U Ranch encompassed 157,900 acres (64,000 hectares), grazing over 10,000 head of cattle.

In just two decades, Stimson, a whisky-drinking man who loved the West and telling tales around the campfire, had risen from drover to become the cattle king of Canada. But his reign was cut short in 1902, when his major eastern partner, Andrew Allan, died and Allan's family sold the operation to Stimson's old U.S. foreman, George Lane, and some Alberta meat packers without consulting the man who made it all possible. Stimson tried to block the sale in the courts, but the new buyers were too politically connected and he failed, so he packed up and took his ranching experience to one of his old customers, railway contractor and president of CP Railway operations, Sir Cornelius Van Horne. That formidable pair collaborated to develop ranch properties in Cuba, but in 1905, Fred Stimson saw opportunity in Mexico City managing investments for foreigners, and since you can never take the cattle out of the rancher, he started a large dairy farm. Stimson stayed in Mexico City until his health gave out; he returned to Canada in 1911 and died the following year.

JOHN WARE
1845–1905
Our First Black Cowboy

John Ware was a South Carolina plantation slave freed by
Abraham Lincoln's Emancipation Proclamation of 1863 during the U.S. Civil War. Ware was good with horses, and he
drifted west to the Montana Territory to work as a cowboy on
cattle ranches. In 1882, he signed on with range boss George
Lane to drive 3000 head up to Fred Stimson's Bar U ranch in
Alberta—the first cattle in the province.

Black cowboys were common in the American West, but
Ware's arrival in Alberta turned a few heads. This didn't
bother Ware, especially after Stimson offered him a wrangler's
job with good pay. During the 1870s, Ware married, claimed

a section of land and started his own ranch, but he found little success.

In 1888, working once again for Stimson's Bar U ranch, Ware stopped at a spring to water his horse, and, noticing a shiny slick on the surface, he tossed in a match and the spring exploded. Some months later, he would find oil seepage at a farm in Turner Valley, and today, Ware is credited with the discovery of one of Alberta's greatest oil resources. It was also one of the strangest because the Turner Valley find was wet gas, a mixture of oil and natural gas that could be used by vehicles without refining.

John Ware could ride any horse and was so good with a rifle that Fred Stimson recruited him to be a member of his militia to protect his ranch against the Métis. Ware was also as strong as an ox and popularized steer wrestling to the point that it became an event in the Calgary Stampede. Not that Ware ever got to attend the Stampede, because in 1902, his horse stepped into a gopher hole and pitched over onto John, breaking his neck.

Ware's funeral was held in Calgary, and the entire city turned out to pay tribute to the wonderful new Canadian who defied prejudice to help lay the foundations of Alberta's great cattle industry.

GEORGE LANE
1856–1925
Our Third King of Cattle

George Lane was the epitome of a Wild West cowboy. Before leaving Montana in 1884 to become foreman at Fred Stimson's new Bar U ranch, Lane had been a pistol-packing dispatch rider for the U.S. Army, and while still in his teens, he had apprenticed himself to some of the biggest ranchers in Montana to learn the cattle business.

Lane rose to the forefront of Alberta ranchers some years after leaving the Bar U in 1887. He became a cattle buyer and shipper, acquired several ranches and, by 1900, was Alberta's cattle king. However, the best was still to come, and in 1902, Lane partnered with the Winnipeg firm of Gordon, Ironside and Fares to buy the Bar U from the estate of its major shareholder, the late Andrew Allan. The cowboy from Montana, by then a Canadian citizen, controlled over 250,000 acres (101,000 hectares) of land and grazed anywhere from 16,000 to 18,000 head of prime beef. Big, weird, wonderful and becoming very rich, Lane still loved to ride the range with his cowboys and bed down under starry skies. He liked the cowboy life so much that in 1912, along with fellow ranchers Pat Burns, A.E. Cross and Archie McLean, he put up money for the first Calgary Stampede.

Although the Bar U ranch land has now mostly been sold to farms, the ranch itself, with its more than 30 buildings, has been maintained by the Canadian government as a historic site and is worth a trip to see.

ALFRED ERNEST "A.E." CROSS
1861–1932
He Gave Us Suds and the Calgary Stampede

Born in Montréal, Alfred Ernest Cross trained as veterinary surgeon before moving to Alberta in 1884 to practise his chosen profession. Two years later, Cross had his own ranch, the A7 Ranche on Mosquito Creek near Nanton, Alberta.

Cross loved ranching, but the financial returns were less than stellar, and when an attack of appendicitis provided him with

an excuse to return to Montréal for surgery, he switched horses midstream and learned the art of brewing beer. In 1891, he was back in Alberta and opened the Calgary Brewing and Malting Company, the West's first commercial brewery. The venture was a financial success and enabled Cross to become a founding member of the ultra-exclusive Ranchmen's Club that same year. If walls could talk, they would tell stories of late-evening suppers and whispered conversations that affected every aspect of western political and economic planning. Calgary was the heart of the Canadian West, and the Ranchmen's Club was the brain. It was over a dinner there that Cross, big-time cattlemen George Lane and Patrick Burns, and rancher and political pundit Archie McLean got the idea for the Calgary Stampede.

With demand for his beer skyrocketing, Cross expanded the factory, and to facilitate his commute from the ranch and provide visitors and salesmen with a place to hang their hats, he bought a nearby hotel—he eventually owned about 50 hotels across four provinces.

In 1889, Cross threw his hat into the political arena, becoming a Conservative member of the provincial legislature, and married Rothney Macleod, daughter of the famous lawman Colonel James F. Macleod. Whatever Cross touched turned to gold, literally, because one of his properties turned up that valuable metal in large quantities. Gold mining was so successful that he formed other companies to search for other minerals and to drill for oil and gas as well. A.E. Cross, a weird and wonderful Canadian, only wanted to enjoy life but acquired a pile of money in the process.

DAVID A. DUNLAP
1863–1924
Milk as Good as Gold

David Dunlap was born poor, died very rich and in between used the wealth he acquired from gold mines in Timmins and Cobalt to buy 600 acres (243 hectares) west of the Don River and south of York Mills Road. In 1914, David and his wife, Jesse Donalda Bell, established Donalda Farms, a dairy farm that, for the times, was something of a miracle. Hundreds of Guernsey cows lived in scrupulously clean, tiled barns, munching the best fodder that money could buy while listening to piped-in classical music. Mothers could give their kids milk from Donalda Farms without fearing that it was diseased, and the farm prospered like no other until properties in the area were subdivided in the 1950s for home construction.

Even after contributing millions to the Toronto General Hospital and the Art Gallery of Ontario, Dunlap left an estate worth more than $6 million. His home on Donalda Crescent, which once overlooked verdant cow pastures, is now the clubhouse of the Donalda Golf and Country Club and over-looks a verdant fairway.

COUGAR ANNIE
1888–1985
Hard as Nails with a Heart as Big as a Garden

Cougar Annie was born Ada Annie Jordan in Sacramento, California, and arrived at Boat Basin in the far reaches of Hesquiat Harbour on Vancouver Island's isolated west coast in 1915, along with an opium-addicted husband and three children. A self-sufficient woman, Annie did whatever was necessary to provide for her family—she cleared land for goats and chickens, ran a trapline, planted a garden to raise produce and shot cougars and bears for the bounty money. She got so good at bagging cougars that the locals began call-ing her "Cougar Annie," a name that stuck for her entire life.

Annie's husband died in 1936, so she advertised in newspapers for another, a process she would repeat three times before run-ning the last one off at gunpoint. She had eight more children by these mail-order hubbies because she loved kids as much as she loved gardening. Annie opened a small general store dur-ing the 1920s, and in 1936, she added a post office, but all the while she was experimenting with flower bulbs and testing the land to see what grew best. In 1942, she witnessed the Japanese shelling of the Estevan Lighthouse and claimed that she actually saw the submarine surface in Hesquiat Harbour before it lobbed 25 or so shells at the lighthouse, but she was more afraid that it would shell her precious gardens.

Cougar Annie was quite a woman, a real wild and wonderful character probably best remembered for those sprawling gar-dens. Over the years, with help from her children and the odd volunteer, she cleared much more land, about 5 acres

(2 hectares), and her major source of income became selling flower bulbs (mostly hybrid dahlias) and other plants by mail across the nation.

In 1985, after Annie had passed away, a long-time friend and admirer, retired Vancouver stockbroker Peter Buckland, bought the gardens from her estate and spent 15 years restoring them to their former glory, creating a living memorial to Cougar Annie. Today, her gardens are a joy to behold and are still there for all to enjoy.

CHARLES SHERWOOD NOBLE
1873–1957
A Farmer for All Seasons

Originally from Iowa, Charlie Noble moved to Alberta to farm a homestead. Not content with remaining small, he began buying land, and by 1918, Charlie was farming over 30,000 acres (12,000 hectares) and had founded the town of Nobleford.

Four years later, in 1922, a drought resulted in his land being repossessed by the bank, and he lost everything. However, Charlie, now a Canadian citizen, went to work getting his land back, and by 1930, he was farming 8000 acres (3200 hectares). He farmed in Alberta's dry belt, an area prone to soil erosion by wind, and during a 1935 trip to California, he noticed sugar beet farmers tilling fields with a straight-blade plow that killed weeds without disturbing the soil. Back in Nobleford, Charlie experimented with the plow and came up with a design that worked wonders on dry-belt soil. He took out a patent on his invention, and calling it the Noble Blade, went from farmer to industrialist by sending his plough worldwide from a factory in Nobleford. Touted as one of the greatest agricultural inventions of the 20th century, the Noble Blade made Charlie rich enough to buy back his remaining lost acreage and a lot more.

JOHN WALTER "GRANT" MacEWAN
1902–2000
He Taught Science to Our Farmers

In 1921, Brandon, Manitoba, native Grant MacEwan had a yen to make himself a better farmer, so he cleaned out his bank account and left the family farm to enroll at Ontario's University of Guelph. He got a master's degree and returned west to Saskatchewan, where he got a travelling job with the University of Saskatchewan, teaching farmers what he had learned about being a better farmer.

During the dustbowl days of the 1930s, he convinced some farmers to plant Russian thistle, and those that did saved their

soil and had fodder for their animals. Prairie farmers in desperate financial straits were killing horses in huge numbers with the meat going to waste, so MacEwan had a party and served horsemeat sandwiches to unsuspecting guests, a trick that backfired and for which he was never forgiven. In the midst of that terrible time, MacEwan took to writing about animals, western lore and farming, and he made such a reputation for himself that in 1948, the University of Manitoba offered him a job as dean of agriculture.

In 1950, when the Red River flooded and destroyed much of Winnipeg, MacEwan was everywhere, saving animals, heaping sandbags and behaving pretty much like a man should, for which he got his picture in the paper and had to endure accusations of publicity seeking from his fellow educators. Shortly afterward, he ran in a by-election against seasoned politician Walter Dinsdale. MacEwan was defeated soundly, but he had caught the political bug, and when an alderman's seat became vacant on the Calgary city council, he moved there and won the seat. In 1963, MacEwan went after the office of mayor of Calgary and won, but he immediately alienated fellow council members with his thrifty policies, though these endeared him to citizens, especially his daily bus rides to work and chats with other riders.

MacEwan began writing again, penning biographies of western heroes: Louis Riel, the black cowboy John Ware and the pioneering grandmother Marie-Anne Gaboury. In 1965, while working on a new book, he received a phone call from John Diefenbaker during which the prime minister asked Grant to become the lieutenant-governor of Alberta.

MacEwan served as lieutenant governor from 1966 to 1974 and did exactly what he had done during his first job as an educator—he took himself to the people of Alberta and they loved him for it. Shortly after taking on the position, Queen

Elizabeth invited him to lunch with her aboard the Royal Yacht *Britannia* in the Vancouver harbour, an invitation he had to decline because of a previous commitment to attend a Boy Scout supper. He mentored politicians and made time for anyone who wanted to visit his office, offering guests cookies from a big jar he kept on his desk.

A grateful province named all kinds of things after MacEwan, but most important to him was Grant MacEwan Community College, now a university. On his final visit to the college, Greyhound sent the bus they had named the *Grant MacEwan* to pick him up, and when they wheeled MacEwan from the seniors' home onto the coach, the crowd clapped and cheered, and there was not a dry eye among them.

Grant MacEwan was the people's politician, everyone's grand-father and a truly wonderful Canadian.

DID YOU KNOW?

Unlike the U.S., Canada does not require its politicians to divulge their religious affiliations. A U.S. politician would find election to public office impossible without constituents know-ing his or her religion, but Canadians do not seem to care. According to occasional surveys conducted by on-the-street pollsters, 99 percent of Canadians have no idea which religion the leaders of major political parties practise, including the current prime minister, Stephen Harper.

The answer to the question of Stephen Harper's religious affiliation? He is a member of the Christian and Missionary Alliance, an evangelical church.

The Railroaders

Never in the history of Canada would such an opportunity for graft and corruption present itself as it did with the building of the Canadian Pacific transcontinental railway. Every politician from the prime minister on down lined up to fill their pockets through kickbacks from the project's initial contractors. The contractors colluded with one another in submitting grossly inflated construction quotes, agents of surveyors arranged track deviations for a price, which allowed land speculators to reap huge profits, and stock promoters diddled investors out of millions. Over a five-year period, with millions of dollars spent, the railway had only progressed a few hundred kilometres and its future, along with that of the country, looked doubtful.

The government of Sir John A. Macdonald, who was "caught lining his pockets, but forgiven by voters," needed to find a man inured to graft and

corruption, which they did—an American named William Cornelius Van Horne, who completed the railway on time and within budget. It was a blip in the norm, though, as graft and corruption had become so ingrained within the Canadian economic system that almost all new projects, especially railways, required the greasing of several palms. In major cities, labourers wanting jobs on the railway had to pay labour recruiters, while the recruiters paid off aldermen, who then split the kickbacks with councilmen or legislators. New mines, industries and lumber ventures requiring a rail line or spur had to pay the right people, and getting a station for an outlying town could cost a fortune. No matter— if a speculator had the inside track on tracks, he could buy and flip land and make a fortune in the process, and many did just that.

SIR CASAMIR GZOWSKI
1813–98
The Man Who Built It All

Deported to the U.S. after the abortive 1830 Polish uprising against Russian authority, Gzowski learned first law and then engineering, and applied his skills to building canals and roads. In 1841, Gzowski journeyed to Kingston in a bid to acquire the Welland Canal building contract, and though he failed in that respect, he so impressed Governor Charles Bagot that he was offered and accepted the position of Superintendent of Roads and Waterways for the Hamilton area. Gzowski built roads, canals and the harbours of Port Stanley and Rondeau. In 1845, working mostly out of Toronto, he joined a mining syndicate to explore and develop copper mines.

In 1849, the passage of the Guarantee Act by the province opened up opportunities for railways, and Gzowski was hired by St. Lawrence and Atlantic Railway director Alexander Galt to run a rail line from Toronto to Sarnia. That led to other lucrative railway contracts, and in 1854, Gzowski & Company won the contract to build the Toronto Esplanade; however, the deal fell apart because of accusations of contract padding, and Gzowski and Alexander Galt parted ways. Undaunted, Gzowski & Company soldiered on, building more rail lines and acquiring various waterfront businesses such as cotton and whale oil companies, an iron-rolling mill and the Rossin Hotel.

In 1870, Gzowski performed his engineering swan song— building the railway bridge across the Niagara River. In 1879, after serving both the federal and provincial governments in various advisory roles, he was appointed aide-de-camp to Queen Victoria and was knighted in 1890.

JAMES JEROME HILL
1838–1916
The Canadian Empire Builder

Born in Rockwood, Ontario, James Hill left school in 1852 when his father died but obtained a recommendation from his principal for his proficiency in mathematics. In 1858, wanting to try his hand at fur trapping, Hill headed to St. Paul, Minnesota, but he arrived too late in the season and had to settle for a job as a freight agent for a steamboat company. When the U.S. Civil War broke out in 1861, Hill volunteered to fight but was refused because a childhood accident had left him blind in his right eye. Undeterred, he formed the 1st Minnesota Volunteers, and though his company saw no action, they were instrumental in forwarding supplies of hay to Union forces.

While engaged in this military service, Hill learned the financial intricacies of supply, demand and fast delivery. Railways were the answer, and after the war, he signed on as an agent for the St. Paul & Pacific Railroad Company. Thinking that coal was a better fuel for locomotives than wood, Hill partnered with a Connecticut wholesale grocer to supply both coal and food to St. Paul, establishing the first of his monopolies. The St. Paul & Pacific moved supplies west, but not as far as the Pacific and not to any place important such as the Hudson's Bay post at Fort Garry (present-day Winnipeg). If Hill had his way, the railway would go to Fort Garry *and* be profitable.

In 1873, Hill got his chance when the St. Paul & Pacific went into receivership. He went to Montréal and convinced both the Hudson's Bay Company and the Bank of Montreal to each buy half of the railway. To make it profitable, he purchased new rolling stock and had crews laying a mile of track per day to connect with the incomplete Canadian Pacific line to Fort Garry. Hill soon found himself a director of CP and was the man responsible for recommending William Cornelius Van Horne as manager. However, still intending to run his own railway to the Pacific, he resigned from the CP board in 1882 and returned to St. Paul to begin construction westward.

Hill employed 8000 men to lay track and build bridges, and by 1886, his rail line ran into the Dakotas. He enticed immigrants to settle near his tracks by offering cheap land and almost-free transportation. In 1893, his railway, now called the Great Northern, reached Puget Sound on the west coast. Hill knew that lumber would be shipped east and that meant empty cars returning, so he sent scouts all through the northern and southeastern U.S. to source products to ship west.

During hard times, Hill gave free cattle and seed grain to farmers and lowered tariffs. As a result, more than 6 million

acres (2.4 million hectares) of the Montana Territory was settled in a little over two years. In 1905, the battle between the
Union Pacific and the Great Northern began over control of
the Oregon Country, with tracks and bridges being dynamited
and running gunfights, but in the end, James Hill took control of the Spokane, Portland and Seattle Railway, making
him the last of the great railway moguls.

SIR WILLIAM CORNELIUS VAN HORNE
1843–1915
The Right Man for a Big Job

Back in power in 1878, Sir John A. Macdonald had only three
years remaining on his Confederation agreement to connect
British Columbia to the rest of Canada by railway. In a panic,

Sir John searched for someone like himself—a man with plenty of gall and few scruples—and found William Cornelius Van Horne, the superintendent of the Illinois Central Railway.

In 1881, Van Horne took on the almost impossible task of completing the rail line and succeeded beyond all expectations. He became president of the CPR in 1888 and turned his attention to doing what he loved best—castle building. An amateur architect, gardener and a colourful character, Van Horne became the preeminent castle builder of his time, constructing magnificent edifices such as the Château Frontenac, the Banff Springs Hotel, the Château Lake Louise and many smaller-but-still-grand hotels, all surrounded by magnificent gardens.

DID YOU KNOW?

Pierre Salinger, press secretary to U.S. president John F. Kennedy, lived in Toronto at 37 Lonsdale Road as a child, while author Farley Mowat lived down the road at 90 Lonsdale for a few years. In the middle, at 83 Lonsdale, novelist Joy Fielding practised her golf stroke and worked on her bestsellers.

Our Sports People

Canada is a nation that invites participation in sports like no other on the planet—there are millions of lakes and rivers for water sports, plenty of ice and snow with hills and mountains for skiers and climbers, and our lush forests beckon campers, hikers and adventurers. Canadians have always been active people, and if they are not doing the aforementioned, they're inventing a new sport such as basketball or baseball.

The invention of basketball is probably no surprise to readers, as almost everyone knows about Canadian Dr. James Naismith and his two peach baskets. However, not many will know that the first recorded baseball game was not played at Cooperstown in 1839 as is recorded in most history books, but at Beachville, a small village in Oxford County, Ontario, a fact attested to by respected Denver physician Dr. Adam E. Ford in an 1886 letter to Sporting Life *magazine.*

Dr. Ford, who was born in Beachville and was present at the games, outlined the rules of the same game played at Cooperstown in 1839 and added in his letter that baseball had been played in Beachville for many years before 1839. Dr. Ford's letter is the first formal account of the game of baseball, and it flies in the face of U.S. claims to that invention.

EDWARD "NED" HANLAN
1855–1908
He Rowed Canada onto the World Map

Bootlegger, hotelier and one of the greatest sports figures of the 19th century, Ned Hanlan, the "boy in blue" and world champion single-scull rower, put Canada on the world map like no other athlete before him. His father, John, one of the Toronto Islands' earliest residents and its first constable, constructed a small hotel on the eastern tip of the peninsula at a place that came to be called Hanlan's Point.

By order of the Toronto city council, no alcoholic beverages were allowed on the Toronto Islands, but going without meant fewer customers, so John Hanlan defied the law and offered clients a full bar of bootlegged spirits. His youngest son, Ned, was the bootlegger's runner and got in plenty of rowing practice ferrying cases of whisky over from the mainland. Ned also rowed back and forth to school, fetched groceries for the hotel and pretty much spent all his time at the oars. That was fine by Ned. He got very good at rowing, a tremendously popular spectator sport in those days, and he was soon beating all comers at Island regattas. In 1873, Ned won the championship of Toronto Bay, and the following year, wearing his trademark blue shirt and red headband for the first time, Ned beat famous Ontario sculler Thomas Loudan in a race that featured a side bet of $100. A year later, he won the Ontario championship and even more money from side bets.

The sport was now attracting sizeable prize money and the side bets caught the attention of Toronto businessmen, who formed a syndicate to back Ned's ambition to be the world's best and make some money in the process. Ned won all his races, earning a small fortune for himself and a large one for his syndicate, but in 1878, the amount of money became obscene when a large group of wealthy Torontonians wagered $300,000 (around $30 million today) on Ned's bid to become the United States rowing champion. He won handily, which earned him a hero's reception on his return to Toronto. The next year, he defeated the English champion and got another hero's welcome. However, his welcome of welcomes occurred in 1880 after he defeated Australian E.A Trikett for the world rowing championship.

Ned Hanlan would go on to win another 300 matches, only losing six in his career, and he is remembered by a statue on Hanlan's Point, close to where he constructed his famous Hanlan's Hotel in 1880.

ÉTIENNE DESMARTEAU
1873–1905
He Defied Authority and Tossed Canada an Olympic Gold

Born in Boucherville, Québec, Étienne Desmarteau moved to Montréal in his teens. In 1901, he joined the police department as well as the Montréal Athletic Club, where he excelled at throwing the 50-pound (23-kilogram) weight, a once immensely popular sport. A year later, Desmarteau became the American Athletic Union champion when he beat John Flanagan with a record throw, but he was bested by Flanagan in 1903, one year before the Summer Olympics in St. Louis, Missouri.

Confident that he could beat Flanagan and win Canada its first Olympic medal, Desmarteau applied to the police department for a leave of absence and received a definite "*Non*." Knowing that it would cost him his job, Desmarteau cleaned out his bank account to pay for travel and other expenses and went anyway, defeating Flanagan soundly and winning what was thought at the time to be Canada's first Olympic gold.

(This honour was later reattributed to Canadian runner George Orton, who won a gold at the 1900 Olympics while competing for the U.S. team.) Étienne Desmarteau was the people's hero, and his return to Montréal featured a grand parade, a medal and a promotion by the police department— with no mention of his being fired.

HAROLD BALLARD
1903–90
As Mean as a Junkyard Dog But a Big Part of Canada's Game

The Beatles' 1965 appearance at Maple Leaf Gardens coincided with a Toronto heat wave, and to capitalize financially on the weather, the Gardens' part owner and general manager, Harold Ballard, ordered his staff to turn on the heat, shut off all the drinking fountains and triple the price of soft drinks. That was Ballard before 1972, the year he schemed his way to full ownership of both the Toronto Maple Leafs and the Gardens and then was carted off to prison for a few years for misappropriating funds.

In 1973, after having served one-third of his sentence, Ballard bought the Hamilton Tiger-Cats football club, and though they were a winning team, Ballard still called his footballers "overpaid losers." In 1978, he infuriated the public by dumping the much-loved "voice of hockey," Foster Hewitt, and tossing the famed announcer's orange broadcast gondola onto the trash heap.

Ballard's bad-boy antics were enabled by Toronto Maple Leafs fans, who, despite being cramped, victimized and having to back a team weakened by bad trades and Ballard selling off the talent, still packed the Gardens at every game. Irascible, cranky and mean as a junkyard dog, Ballard became the most despised man in the history of organized sport. Not that it mattered to him—he had his Georgian Bay cottage for peace and quiet and time to plan his next outrage while he built birdhouses. Harold Ballard died there in 1990, in a cottage surrounded by trees festooned with empty birdhouses, and his last words were, "I'm going now."

JACK KENT COOK
1912–97
He Could Sell Anything

Born in Hamilton, Ontario, and raised in The Beaches area of Toronto, Jack Cook sold encyclopedias door to door to help bolster family finances. After graduating from high school, he became a runner on the floor of the Toronto Stock Exchange. Sensing little future in that endeavour, he went to work for Colgate Palmolive, peddling soap in hard-to-sell areas of northern Ontario, where his gift for gab attracted the attention of future media mogul Roy Thompson.

Thompson hired Cook to run a radio station in Stratford, Ontario, and the pair got on so famously that they became partners in 1941, with Cook doing the preliminaries to buying new radio stations and local newspapers. In 1946, with the backing of financer J.P. Bickel, Cook bought what would become an iconic Toronto radio station, CKEY. Two years later, he and Bickel bought a national media icon, *Liberty* magazine, with Cook selling his share to Thompson the following year. Cook had a yen for the business of sport, and in 1951, he bought the minor league Toronto Maple Leafs baseball club, intending to transform it into a major league team, something he accomplished in 1959. Television was next, and when his bid to start Toronto's first TV station failed, he showed his pique by moving to the U.S., where, through an act of Congress, he became an immediate citizen.

In Los Angeles, Cook purchased the Lakers basketball team and set about bringing Canada's national sport of hockey to the City of Angels. A good bet, since he had been told there were 300,000 expat Canadians living in the Los Angeles area. But in 1979, when hardly anyone showed up to watch his new franchise, the Los Angeles Kings, play in the newly constructed Forum, he said, "Now I know why they left Canada. They hate hockey." He sold the works and turned to raising horses and tending to his marital difficulties.

Cook collected wives like they were sports franchises and had a total of five, though he married one woman twice, Marlene Chalmers, 40 years his junior and purported to be a former drug runner for a Bolivia cartel. Two of his marriages lasted only a few months but cost him millions.

MURRAY IRWIN "MOE" NORMAN
1929–2004
King of the Golf Swing

Born in Kitchener, Ontario, and with the attributes to become the world's greatest golfer, Moe Norman suffered one serious roadblock to fame—autism. Like many other autistics, Moe had a gift, not of musical ability, but in the swing of a golf club, and it was not a swing that golfers aspire to emulate—it looked like he was swinging a sledgehammer.

When Moe took his ugly swing on the Canadian pro tour in 1966, he won five of the 12 tournaments, came in second in five others and amazed both spectators and players with his ability to keep the ball on target. Winning would be a lifelong problem for Moe because his autism caused him to be deathly

afraid of celebrity; after winning one Canadian tournament, he hid out in the scrub along a riverbank to keep from having to accept the trophy and give a speech.

During his career, in which he won more than 50 tournaments, Moe had 17 hole-in-one shots, 9 double-eagles and set 30 course records. After winning a tournament, Moe would cash his cheque and stash the bills in the trunk of his car next to cases of Coke. Moe drank lots of Coca-Cola, a case of 24 every day, and he would have been a natural for advertising were it not for his aversion to publicity.

Tournament star Lee Trevino once said that Moe had come into the game too early, "Had he come in later, he would have had an agent and handlers to insulate him from the anxiety of public life."

And Tiger Woods, probably the greatest golfer of all time, said, "Only two players have owned their swings, Ben Hogan and Moe Norman."

MANDY-RAE CRUICKSHANK
1974–
Our Beauty of the Deeps

Edmonton, Alberta, native Mandy-Rae Cruickshank is as cute as button and can hold her breath for over six minutes. She is also the star and cover girl for the documentary film *The Cove*. Mandy's specialty is freediving, a sport in which she holds 13 Canadian records and seven world records. Her personal bests include a no-limits freedive to 136 metres and a constant-weight, world-record dive to 88 metres.

Together with her husband, fellow Canadian and freediver Kirk Krack, Mandy is part of the Performance Freediving International instructors team, a group that has trained over 3000 freedivers from around the globe. So many going to a place that so few want to go is perhaps because of Mandy's influence—did I mention that she's cute? Well, maybe not at 88 metres.

JORDIN TOOTOO
1983–
A Tough Nut from Nunavut

It is a long way from Rankin Inlet, Nunavut, to Tennessee, where Jordin Tootoo plays hockey for the Nashville Predators. He is the first Inuit to play in the NHL and is what Don Cherry calls a "rock 'em, sock 'em" player.

Signed by the Predators in 2006, Jordin re-signed in 2008 with a $1 million salary and re-signed again in 2010 for $2 million. The young man was living large, with fast cars, celebrity dates and plenty of martinis, but his social excesses began to show during games, when rock 'em, sock 'em turned to cheap shots and game suspensions. These were hardly the actions of a role model for the kids in Nunavut, so in January 2011, Jordin became the first Inuit to enter the NHL rehab program and has successfully returned to fair play on the ice and is once again a shining example for the kids back home.

DID YOU ▮ KNOW?

In the early days of hockey, a favourite trick of spectators was to toss pieces of coal shaped like hockey pucks onto the ice. The sudden appearance of so many pucks would confuse the opposing team and stop play faster than the octopuses and rubber rats tossed onto the ice during modern-day hockey games.

CLARENCE SUTHERLAND CAMPBELL
1905–84
He Gave His All to the National Game

In the early 20th century, Fleming, Saskatchewan, offered little in the way of diversion, except hockey. Study, play hockey and get ready for college was all she wrote for Clarence Campbell. He was more than ready for the University of Alberta, where he played hockey, got a law degree and was good enough at both to be accepted to England's Oxford University as a Rhodes Scholar, where he played hockey for the Oxford Blues.

A good player but not great, Campbell eschewed chasing a player's jersey for a job as an NHL referee, where he officiated some rough-and-tumble games. In one such matchup between the Montréal Maroons and the Boston Bruins, he swore at Bruins player Dit Clapper for high sticking and got punched out. In 1939, he blew an important call and was banned from refereeing by Leafs owner Con Smyth and demoted to doing office work for the NHL.

With the war in Europe turning ugly, Campbell volunteered and mustered out as a colonel, even doing a stint as a prosecutor at the Nuremberg Trials. After returning to Canada in 1946, he moved from doing office work to the NHL presidency when Red Dutton resigned over a dispute with the NHL executive. Campbell had disputes also, but he was not averse to engaging in boardroom wrestling matches to decide important issues. Stubborn as a pitbull and not a bit shy, he ignored police warnings after his controversial 1955 season ban of Rocket Richard and showed up at the Montréal Forum for a game, precipitating the infamous Richard Riots in which he narrowly missed being strung up by rampaging fans.

Campbell was also not averse to greasing palms and wasn't caught in the act until 1976, when the Mounties charged him with bribing Senator Louis Giguère in what became known as the "Sky Shops Affair." Campbell was convicted but escaped a jail sentence because of his connections and his advanced age. Campbell retired a sick man in 1977, having given his all to our national sport, and he passed away in 1984.

DID YOU KNOW?

The world's second oldest hockey club is not located in Canada, but at England's Oxford University. Formed in 1885 and called the Oxford University Ice Hockey Club, or the Oxford Blues, the team has, over the years, featured many top Canadian players, most of them being Rhodes Scholars. Canadians on the Oxford roster have included Lester B. Pearson, Roland Michener, historian and Canadian flag designer George F.G. Stanley, Clarence Campbell and Supreme Court Justice Ron Martland.

DONALD STEWART "DON" CHERRY
1934–
Not Quite the Greatest Canadian

As the greatest booster in the history of hockey, Don "Grapes" Cherry has no equal, and while Foster Hewitt had the voice, Don Cherry is the face, coat, mouth and shirt-collar icon of Canada's national game. Unrelenting, obnoxious, ranting and an unabashed fan of "rock 'em, sock 'em" hockey, the guy is constantly itching for a fight while trying to sell us something. Don Cherry is an "Uncle Sam Wants You" poster come alive, and Canadians love the image enough to have voted him number seven in the Greatest Canadian contest run by the CBC in 2004.

Mister Hockey is as hard as nails but has an Achilles heel that defies his tough-guy image. The truth is that Cherry has a heart much bigger than his mouth and has devoted so much of himself to helping sick kids and their families that it is a miracle he has any energy left to irritate the public into buying stuff. In 2004, after 10 years of raising something great from nothing, Cherry opened the Rose Cherry Home, a hospice for sick children, on the escarpment above the town of Milton—and everyone in attendance got to see Canada's hockey tough guy cry real tears.

PETER HUGH "PUCK" POCKLINGTON
1941–
Button, Button, Who's Got the Button?

Best known for his ownership of Wayne Gretzky and the Edmonton Oilers, Peter "Puck" Pocklington is a London, Ontario, born financial wizard who flew high and crashed hard during the 1990s. The Puck started out selling used cars, then new cars, and during the mid-1970s, he cobbled together a diverse empire of food, trust and sports companies that included his grandest acquisition, the Edmonton Oilers hockey franchise. Pocklington could do no wrong in Edmonton until he sold Wayne Gretzky to the Los Angeles Kings, a deed that would see him burned in effigy. Nobody could understand the reason for such an unfathomable move until the sheriff came calling to seize all of Peter Puck's stuff—his companies, his private jet, his Renoirs and Group of Seven paintings, his Cuban cigars and his million-dollar wine collection. It all went to pay his creditors, while Peter Puck hightailed it to Las Vegas to wait out the storm.

Gone but not down, Pocklington left behind one memento that not many know about—the infamous series of *X*s on the Stanley Cup. When the Oilers won their first Stanley Cup at the end of the 1983–84 season, Pocklington slipped his dad's name into the list of people to be engraved onto the cup. A nice touch, but when the NHL found out, they had the name crossed out.

Don't pity poor Peter too much, though, since the guy is still living the good life in Las Vegas while making periodic tries at a comeback.

WAYNE DOUGLAS GRETZKY
1961–
The Great One

Born in Brantford, Ontario, Gretzky grew up under the tute-lage of his father, Walter, who flooded the family's backyard every winter so young Wayne could practise his burgeoning hockey skills. The extra effort paid off, because Wayne was playing with 10-year-olds when he was six. He was drafted by the Sault Ste. Marie Greyhounds in 1977, where he first started wearing his trademark jersey number 99.

His size and stature, however, were cause for criticism—many NHL scouts believed the young phenom would not be able to withstand the physical rigours of professional hockey. Nelson Skalbania, owner of the flailing Indianapolis Racers, felt other-wise and offered the 17-year-old a four-year contract that would pay him $1.125 million.

When the Racers folded, Peter Pocklington, owner of the WHA Edmonton Oilers, bought the rights to Gretzky. The young Gretzky's WHA debut was so impressive that on January 26, Wayne's 18th birthday, Pocklington signed the youngster to a new contract valued at approximately $5 million, which would keep Gretzky in Edmonton until 1999. "Looks like I'm here for life," he said at the time.

In 1987, Wayne met Janet Jones, a beautiful actress, at a Los Angeles Lakers game. After a fast and furious courtship, they were married in Edmonton in August 1988. However, Wayne's days with the Oilers were numbered. Only a day after the team won its fourth Stanley Cup, Pocklington told Gretzky that he was going to be traded. Pocklington was in dire need of cash, and Gretzky was his most valuable asset.

August 9, referred to in Edmonton as "Black Sunday," was the day Pocklington convened a press conference in which Wayne told the media that it was his idea to be traded to the Los Angeles Kings (many Edmontonians blamed Janet for the move).

Gretzky played with the Kings until 1996, and, after a brief stint with the St. Louis Blues, finished his playing career with the New York Rangers, retiring in April 1999. He was inducted into the Hockey Hall of Fame in 1999. In the summer of 2000, he became a minority owner of the Phoenix Coyotes, and that November, he was named executive director of Canada's 2002 men's Olympic hockey team.

Gretzky gives his time to numerous charitable organizations, in particular the Wayne Gretzky Foundation, which is dedicated to helping disadvantaged youngsters throughout North America participate in hockey. He is also the father of five children: daughters Paulina and Emma and sons Ty, Trevor and Tristan.

DID YOU KNOW?

In 1981, Gretzky appeared in an episode of the TV soap opera *The Young and the Restless*.

DARYL ALLAN KATZ
1962–
Our Hockey High Roller

Daryl Katz (pronounced "Cates") might have been a hockey player if not for his pharmacist father. After graduating from the University of Alberta with a law degree, Daryl asked his dad "Now what?" and was thrown a bottle of pills. Young Daryl was broke, so he visited the head office of pharmaceutical giant McKesson with an idea to buy poorly performing drugstore chains and turn them around. By 1995, bankrolled by McKesson, Daryl had assembled almost 1900 drugstores. Under Daryl's management, those drugstores began turning huge profits, and by the start of the millennium, the young man was a billionaire.

So what does an Edmonton billionaire who really wanted to be a hockey player do with all that money? Why, he buys himself a hockey team, the Edmonton Oilers. Being a first-class kind of guy and wanting the best venue for his new team, Daryl began consulting with architects and city officials about building a new arena and entertainment complex in Edmonton to be called the Katz Centre. Huge projects take time, and while waiting for the city to make a decision, Katz was bitten by the building bug and hired architects to design a house for his wife and two kids—a 25,000-square-foot, modern, steel-and-glass behemoth with a great view and both indoor and outdoor swimming pools. The outside pool doubles as a hockey rink in winter, because if Daryl's kids have any talent for the game, they are definitely going to be hockey players.

Our Mysterious People

*Although being obtuse is almost always explainable
because people usually have a reason for doing what
they do, the weird and mysterious individuals in this
chapter leave us with no rationale for their actions.
Nothing captures the public consciousness like a mystery, and no stone is left unturned trying to answer
the question, "Why would anyone do such a thing?"—
a query for which there is seldom a logical answer.*

ALEXIS ST. MARTIN
1794–1880
He Gave Us a Look Inside

In 1822, Canadian voyageur Alexis St. Martin was accidentally shot beneath his left breast at close range by a musket charged with birdshot. The blast tore away parts of his left side, exposing bone, tissue and organs. His stomach was exposed and punctured, and the physician who attended him, Dr. William Beaumont, concluded that St. Martin would soon die. However, he did not die, and though his grievous wound never completely healed, he survived for another 58 years.

Seizing an opportunity to advance medical science, Dr. Beaumont began to use St. Martin as a text subject. He would extract partially digested food from his patient's exposed stomach at various intervals to determine the functions of the organ, which until St. Martin's educationally fortunate accident were only theory. St. Martin was quite happy to expose his innards because he charged doctors for every look and enjoyed a comfortable life, except for having to wear special support underwear.

When St. Martin passed away, the doctors still wanted his innards and offered his relatives a comfortable sum to get them. Thinking it all too silly for consideration, the relatives confounded medical grave robbers by burying St. Martin's remains 2.5 metres deep and filling the grave with stones.

AMBROSE SMALL
1863–1919
A Mousetrap Mystery in Toronto

Whatever happened to Ambrose Small? That question has confounded historians and police since Small vanished on

December 2, 1919. Many Torontonians have disappeared over the years, and though a few have attracted the public's attention, none has created more interest than the disappearance of Grand Opera House owner Ambrose Small. The reason behind the singular interest is the $1.7 million cheque that he deposited in his bank account some hours before he went missing, money that he had received from the sale of his theatre chain.

After depositing the cheque, Small had lunch with his wife, Theresa, and returned to his office at the Grand Opera House. Later that afternoon, he left work, bought a newspaper and walked off into what was, according to a 1936 report by an OPP inspector named Edward Hammond, a murderous trap devised by his wife and his personal secretary, John Doughty.

Inspector Hammond claimed that the case was a cover-up by Toronto police because of Theresa Small's social prominence, but since the officer didn't file his report until a year after Theresa's death in 1935, his theory was regarded as supposition. No trace of Ambrose Small was ever found, and the mystery continues to the present day, but not for the Toronto police, as they grew tired of answering questions about the case from amateur sleuths and reporters and destroyed the file in 1960.

THOMAS JOHN "TOM" THOMSON
1877–1917
Our Premier Painter and Unsolved Mystery

One of the greats of Canadian art, Tom Thomson was an enigma in life as well as death. In 1912, while working at Grip Limited, a Toronto typesetting and lithography company that employed four of the artists who would become known as Canada's Group of Seven, Thomson was advised by his

colleagues to head north for landscape inspiration. The following year, he took the train up to a little station in Algonquin Provincial Park called Joe Lake. From that point on, his artwork took on a whole new dimension, a naturalness that was recognized by his fellow artists, including Lawren Harris, who invited Tom into his sponsored Toronto studio at 25 Severn Street.

In 1914, Thomson tried to enlist as a war artist along with Frederick Varley and A.Y. Jackson, but he was refused and consoled himself by moving to Joe Lake Station, where he produced his best works. In the summer of 1917, Thomson's body was found in Canoe Lake, his legs wrapped in copper fishing line and his head badly bruised. The coroner called it death by drowning and thought that Thomson had hooked onto a big lake trout and during the excitement had stood up in the canoe, tangled his legs in fishing line and fallen into the water, striking his head on a rock.

None of locals believed the verdict—Thomson had been too good with a rod and was so expert a canoeist that he would never have stood up or got his feet tangled. The painter's death was a mystery, one that deepened after his family had his remains dug up and moved to his hometown of Leith, Ontario. In 1956, Judge William Little poked around in what had been Thomson's original gravesite and discovered another body, that of a First Nations man, who, like Thomson, had a cracked skull. However, since only bones were found, it is likely the body was already in the grave before Thomson was buried there.

Although many locals believed that Thomson was murdered by the same person who supposedly overturned his canoe—a local man named Martin Bletcher with whom Thomson had a terrible argument the night before his disappearance—the allegations were never proven. Another theory is that Thomson had gotten into a fight with hotel owner Shannon Fraser over money owed to Thomson. Speculation was that Fraser had struck Thomson, causing him to fall and hit his head on a fire grate. After realizing that the fall had killed his adversary, Fraser, with help from his wife, Anne, hauled Thomson's body to his canoe, wrapped the legs in fishing line and, with Anne following in another canoe, overturned the painter's craft in a remote part of Canoe Lake. Although this scenario remains unsubstantiated, it does carry some weight because Anne Fraser supposedly made a deathbed confession to a friend.

The mysterious death of one of Canada's foremost artists has been the subject of several books and film documentaries and will probably never be solved satisfactorily. However, it has served to add some mystique to Canoe Lake; every season, canoeists report being followed by the spectre of Tom Thomson's canoe-paddling ghost.

MINA STINSON "MARGERY" CRANDON
1888–1941
Our Famous Mistress of Ectoplasmic Shenanigans

She was born Mina Stinson (but was called Margery) in Princeton, a small farming community in southwestern Ontario near Woodstock. In 1901, her father gave up farming and moved the family to Boston, Massachusetts, where he took a job with the railway. It was no life for Margery, and in 1914, she used her charm and good looks to land a husband, Earl P. Rand, a wealthy grocery store owner. That improved her circumstances, but the union lasted only a few years, and in 1918, she hooked and married Dr. Le Roi Goddard Crandon, a man with impeccable social credentials.

Dr. Crandon built Margery a fine home at 10 Lime Street in the Beacon Hill area of Boston, an address that would later prompt magician Harry Houdini to call her "the blonde witch of Lime Street." At the time, psychic research was all the rage and was one of Dr. Crandon's hobbies—during a séance at the Lime Street house, it was revealed that Margery had a spiritual connection with her brother, Walter, who had been killed in a railcar accident 12 years earlier. The excited doctor staged more séances to further investigate Margery's powers and soon found she could stop watches with a look, move objects, speak for the dead and spout ectoplasm like a fountain. Margery's séances became a sensation and put her at the top of Boston's social scene, a situation she improved upon by inventing some fantastic parlour tricks to sway unbelievers, her favourite being a ghostly hand that floated out from between her legs. She was also not above using her good looks to seduce critics, and her sexual liaisons with scientific investigators were suspected but never proven. Margery never charged money for a séance and welcomed scientific investigation, both of which hobbled her detractors and expanded both her fame and numbers of adherents.

In 1924, one of her most vocal critics, Harry Houdini, joined with others in an investigation conducted by *Scientific American* magazine during which it was discovered that Houdini had fixed the tests to the detriment of Margery the Medium, which is what the media had taken to calling Margery. Both Margery and Houdini became the subjects of media ridicule and both lost reputation.

After her husband passed away in 1939, Margery rapidly declined, becoming depressed and turning to alcohol for solace, though she continued to perform until her death.

JOCELYN GORDON WHITEHEAD
1896–1954
The Man Who Killed the Great Houdini

Almost everyone knows that the Great Houdini died of peritonitis from a burst appendix, with the rupture aggravated by a blow to the stomach. Historians have different takes on the tragedy, with some claiming the blow was a sucker punch, while others maintain that Houdini caused his own demise by daring a fan to strike him in the stomach. That fan was first-year McGill University student J. Gordon Whitehead, and as a 30-year-old, trained boxer, he hardly qualified as a student, let alone a fan.

On October 22, 1926, just a few weeks after Whitehead enrolled at the university, Houdini arrived in Montréal to perform at the Princess Theatre. In addition to that engagement, he was also slated to speak to the McGill student body about his sensational exposés of famous spiritualists and mediums. After Houdini gave his talk to the students, two interested lads got an invitation to meet with the magician backstage at the Palace before showtime. At the meeting, one of the students sketched Houdini lying on a sofa—the performer had apparently not been feeling well for weeks. Houdini refused to see a doctor, but his handlers had consulted with one, and the probable diagnosis was acute appendicitis. While the one student sketched and the other chatted with Houdini, there was a knock at the door and when the door opened, there stood J. Gordon Whitehead.

Whitehead had questions about Houdini's reported ability to withstand a punch to the adomen. Houdini said that it was true, his muscles were that well developed, and without another word, Whitehead began to pummel Houdini, not in the stomach, but in the side, and not once, but with a flurry of hard blows. Whitehead had to be pulled off by his fellow students, and it was later revealed that they barely knew the guy.

The Great Houdini died nine days later and all efforts to find J. Gordon Whitehead proved fruitless until years later, when he was found homeless, starving, and unwilling to discuss the matter.

GLENN HERBERT GOULD
1932–82
Our Troubled Maestro of the 88 Keys

Born Glenn Herbert Gold in Toronto, Ontario, the Gold family changed their name to Gould in 1939, about the same time that Glenn began to show promise as musical prodigy. The kid had perfect pitch and could read music like a book, so off he went to study at Toronto's Royal Conservatory of Music, where he absorbed all they could teach and became a professional pianist at only 13 years of age.

In 1946, Gould played with the Toronto Symphony, followed a year later by a solo recital that he repeated in 1950 on CBC Radio, a performance that so enamoured him to the media that he would give up doing public recitals in 1969 to concentrate on radio and recording. In total, he performed on stage about 200 times, during which he progressively became more eccentric. He insisted that concert halls be heated to 26°C, wore winter clothing in summer and developed hypochondria. He stopped appearing in public, shaking hands or touching people, and he drove orchestra conductors mad with his weird body movements and tempo variations. Gould gave his first American recital in 1955 at the Town Hall in New York City, and the next day, he received a recording contract from Columbia Records.

In 1967, he began a five-year affair with noted U.S. sculptress and painter Cornelia Foss, wife of composer Lukas Foss, and while she moved to Toronto into a rented house at 110 St. Clair Avenue, Gould became convinced that Lukas Foss would try to poison him and refused to join her there, preferring the security of his nearby apartment. Cornelia Foss would later describe her time with the pianist as being overly sexual with interludes of extreme paranoia. Besides his increasing paranoia, Gould became even more of a hypochondriac, taking all kinds of prescription medications for what was revealed after his autopsy to be mostly imagined pains and ailments.

On September 27, 1982, complaining of a severe headache and progressive numbness in his extremities, Glenn Gould was admitted to Toronto General Hospital, where the numbness, which was first diagnosed as a stroke, continued to spread. The piano prodigy passed away just a week after his 50th birthday, convinced he had been poisoned.

BERNARD JOHN "BERNIE" EBBERS
1941–
Our Own Bernie Madoff

Born in Edmonton, Alberta, Bernie Ebbers attended the University of Alberta before transferring to Mississippi College in Clinton, Mississippi, on a basketball scholarship. Bernie played a mean game of b-ball and might have made pro if not for an injury that became his proverbial fork in the road. That road eventually led to a 25-year prison sentence for what, until the other Bernie (Madoff) came along, was the swindle of the century.

Fresh out of school, Bernie started running a chain of motels in Mississippi, found the first of his thousands of investors and soon had nine Best Western motels in his portfolio. In 1983, when the U.S. government forced AT&T to divest some of its telephone companies, he found more investors, formed a company named Long Distance Discount Service (LDDS) and bought a money-losing Mississippi telephone company that he quickly had turning a profit. Nothing succeeds like success, and with investors lined up like sheep, Bernie acquired still more telephone companies until he was servicing almost the entire South.

In 1992, he changed the company name from LDDS to WorldCom, acquired more companies through cash and stock and, by 1996, was the fourth-largest long-distance carrier in the U.S. That was also the year he bought MFS Communications and went global, sending his already fast-rising stock into the stratosphere. During media interviews, Bernie loved to expound on his business strategies while dressed in his usual blue jeans and cowboy boots. His technique was to watch the pennies and let the dollars take care of themselves, a practice that had him eschewing expensive restaurants and limos for diners and taxicabs.

It was all very impressive to investors, and the line of sheep grew ever longer, supplying Bernie with the backing to buy MCI Communications in 1997 for $40 billion. "Blue Jean" Bernie was on top of the world, but a failed 1999 attempt to buy Sprint started his slow crumble, and in 2002, he found himself in Chapter 11 bankruptcy. It turns out that Bernie and his accountants had been fudging the books, misrepresenting profits and generally being greedy pigs. The U.S. government sent in their accountants, and while Bernie was enjoying his new ranch near Vancouver, BC, they found that WorldCom had misrepresented its worth to investors by billions of dollars.

Butter didn't melt in Bernie's mouth when he stood in court to solemnly declare his innocence to an unbelieving jury, who, like Bernie Madoff's jury, could not understand why the accused had not run off to some South Seas island nation that didn't have an extradition agreement with Canada. Our weird and naughty Bernie received a 25-year sentence. It's a bit harsh, but sometimes they let him wear his old blue jeans and cowboy boots.

DID YOU KNOW?

James Earl Ray, confessed assassin of famed civil rights leader Dr. Martin Luther King Jr., lived at a rooming house on the west side of Ossington Avenue north of Queen Street in Toronto for several weeks after committing his foul deed on April 4, 1968. While residing in Toronto, on his way to England where he was captured, Ray used the alias Eric S. Galt, a name he probably adopted from the city of Galt, Ontario. Sentenced to 99 years, the confessed murderer would later recant his confession, claiming a plot was instigated by then FBI director Herbert Hoover. His conspiracy claim actually had some merit, and his case was reviewed by the U.S. government but later dismissed as nonsense. James Earl Ray died of liver failure in 1998, still claiming to be Hoover's innocent dupe.

WEIRD, WILD AND WONDERFUL FESTIVALS
Celebrating Our Weirdness

There are numerous festivals that celebrate the unusual in our great country, and they give Canadians the opportunity to exercise their weird, wild and wonderful personas:

☞ At the annual Collingwood Elvis Festival in Collingwood, Ontario, for three days in July, visitors can see as many as 125 Elvis impersonators and celebrate everything Elvis.

☞ In Gimli, Manitoba, visitors can wear horny headgear and go Icelandic at the annual Islendingadagurinn, where drinking mead (honey wine) is encouraged before engaging in activities such as paintball wars.

☞ Every July 24, Grand Prairie, Alberta, hosts an annual extravaganza they call the Down East Garden Party, where visitors learn to drink screech and dance Celtic style.

☞ The annual Star Trek Festival, held every June in Vulcan, Alberta, is a beam-me-up retro experience guaranteed to rattle sensibilities, especially if you happen to meet William Shatner in his pyjama uniform.

☞ In Lamèque, New Brunswick, you can attend the Festival Provincial de la Tourbe each July. What on earth is *la tourbe*? Why, it's peat moss, and the festival celebrates the pioneers and workers in the peat moss industry.

☞ New Brunswick seems to have a plethora of weird and wonderful festivals because you can also take a trip to Rogersville for the Festival des Choux de Bruxelles, which celebrates the humble brussels sprout or hit up Fredericton for the Fiddlehead Festival or travel to Bouctouche for the Festival des Mollusques, which pays homage to various shellfish.

☞ Calling itself the "Chicken Capital of Western Canada," the town of Wynard, Saskatchewan, throws a bash to celebrate all things chicken, including an annual Chicken Chariot Race, while Lumsden sponsors a Duck Derby (with rubber ducks, not real ones) each Labour Day weekend.

ABOUT THE ILLUSTRATORS

Roger Garcia

Roger Garcia is a self-taught artist with some formal training who specializes in cartooning and illustration. He is an immigrant from El Salvador, and during the last few years, his work has been primarily cartoons and editorial illustrations in pen and ink. Recently he has started painting once more. Focusing on simplifying the human form, he uses a bright minimal palette and as few elements as possible. His work can be seen in newspapers, magazines and promo material and on www.rogergarcia.ca

Peter Tyler

Peter Tyler is a recent graduate of the Vancouver Film School's Visual Art and Design and Classical Animation programs. Though his ultimate passion is in filmmaking, he is also intent on developing his draftsmanship and storytelling, with the aim of using those skills in future filmic misadventures.

Patrick Hénaff

Born in France, Patrick Hénaff is mostly self-taught. He is a versatile artist who has explored a variety of media under many different influences. He now uses primarily pen and ink to draw, and then processes the images on computer. He is particularly interested in the narrative power of pictures.

ABOUT THE ILLUSTRATORS

Djordje Todorovic

Djordje Todorovic is an artist/illustrator living in Toronto. He first moved to the city to go to York University to study fine arts. It was there that he got a taste for illustrating while working as the illustrator for the college paper *Mondo Magazine*. He has since worked on various projects and continues to perfect his craft. Aside from his artistic work, Djordje devotes his time to volunteering at the Print and Drawing Centre at the Art Gallery of Ontario. When he is not doing that, he is out trotting the globe.

Roly Wood

Roly Wood has worked in Toronto as a freelance illustrator, and has been employed in the graphic design department of a landscape architecture firm. In 2004, he wrote and illustrated a historical comic book set in Lang Pioneer Village, near Peterborough, Ontario. To see more of Roly's work, visit www.rolywood.com

ABOUT THE AUTHOR

A.H. Jackson

A.H. Jackson believes that in the twine of life, there are two special genes unique to humankind—hope and humour—and he thinks we should all turn to the funny side of life in the face of adversity. He must have quite the sense of humour, then, since he's been struck by lighting five times!

A prolific writer of non-fiction, Jackson is also a creator of worlds in the fiction realm. This is for children, mostly, because they have imaginations unconstrained by reality. Can pigs fly? No, but in one of his books, a pig talks, plots and saves humankind from becoming the bottom link of the food chain.

Jackson lives in Toronto with a wife named "M" and a squirrel called Herbie. He is the author of various non-fiction titles, including four other titles for Blue Bike Books.